GHOST HOLE

AN EPIC POEM

MATT BIALER

LEAKY BOOT PRESS

Ghost Hole: An Epic Poem
by Matt Bialer

ISBN: 978-1-909849-84-6

First published in 2020 by Leaky Boot Press
Copyright © 2020 Matt Bialer

GHOST
HOLE

GHOST
HOLE

In the bedroom

The knockings
Are heard

Through the wall

Through the ceiling

And again
Through the floor

The knockings
Are heard

March 31, 1948

The two younger Fox sisters

Maggie
Age fourteen

Kate
Age eleven

In bed

Frightened

By unexplained sounds

Knockings

Raps

Moving
Of furniture

Farmhouse

In Hydesville,
New York

A town

That no longer exists

No longer exists

Part of the township
Arcadia

Wayne County, NY

Just moved in

With their parents
John and Margaret

Stories around town

House is haunted

Haunted

The knockings are heard

In their pajamas

Puffed sleeves

Frills and ruffles

Soft pink and blue fabrics

Lying in bed together

Chilly dark

Too sleepy

Even to whisper secrets

Whisper secrets

Hear taps

Accuse each other

Of making the sounds

Neither one

Is doing so
But is easier

Less scary

For each child

To believe

Her clever sister

Has invented a game

The night before

April Fool's

Stop teasing me Maggie!
You're scaring me!

I'm not doing it

You are too!

Am not!

The knockings
Are heard

Through the walls

Through the ceiling

And again
Through the floor

The knockings
Are heard

Lying in bed together

Chilly dark

Too sleepy

Even to whisper secrets

Whisper secrets

The girls' mother

Getting ready for bed

A big bang
In the house

Clatter

Their father

Stirs

From his bedside prayer

Mustache

Bushy sideburns

And now Lord

As we lie down

We pray

That you would

Watch over us

To protect

And keep us safe

Stories around town

House is haunted

Haunted

The last people suddenly moved out

The knockings
Are heard

The four of them

Get up

Light candles

Search entire house

But cannot find

A cause

The noise continues

Sudden jars

Footsteps in the pantry

Walking downstairs

The cellar

Mrs. Fox hopes

That it is the wind

It is the wind

Sashes need to be tied

Mr. Fox ties them

Shakes the window sash

The noises

Seem to reply

Katie smiles

Snaps her fingers

Mr. Splitfoot, do as I do!

Claps her hands

Sound

Instantly replies

Same number
Of snaps

When she stops

The sounds cease

Maggie says

No, do just as I do
Count one, two, three, four

Striking

One hand

Against the other

The raps reply

Their mother:

Are you an unsatisfied spirit?

An unsatisfied spirit?

Yes

Oh mother

I know what it is

Tomorrow is April Fool's Day

Somebody is

Trying to fool us!

Are you an unsatisfied spirit?

An unsatisfied spirit?

The knockings
Are heard

Lying in bed together

Chilly dark

Too sleepy

Even to whisper secrets

Whisper secrets

Give us a deep

And refreshing sleep

And may we cast any burdens

Or Difficulties

On You

And not allow

Our minds to fret or worry

For You have promised

To carry all our burdens

If we will just give them to you

In the cellar

Picks and bats

Are at once

Brought into requisition

And in digging down

About four feet

Pure water gushes

And fills up the ghost hole

*****

Mama Mama!
You need to wake up now!

My wife Liz

Turns over in bed

Surprised to see
Our five year old

Charlotte

Blonde
Like her mother

Bright blue eyes

Standing in the doorway

You need to wake up now!

Tara woke me up
And told me

You need to get out of bed

Right now!

She regularly talks

About invisible friend

Tara

Speaks of her
As if she's a special person

Red hair
In a bun

Long white dress

Frills, lace

She's the sort of friend
Nobody can see

Nobody but me
Know what I mean?

Char, go back to bed
You were just having a bad dream

A bad dream

Go back to bed

I won't leave
Until you get out of bed

What's the matter darling?

A bad dream

Tara says
There's a bee on your pillow

A what?
No, there's nothing darling

Just a bad dream

Yes, there is mama
Pull back the covers

And look

More to humor Charlotte
Than anything else

She draws back the quilt

No one more shocked

To see a bee on the pillow

Right next
To where her head lay

There's a bee on your pillow

Char
How did you know this?
How did you know?

She smiles

Closes her eyes

Dances
A circle

And curtsies

Teases

I told ya

Tara told me

Will you thank her?

I want a dress like hers

She's imaginary, invisible
But she's never scary

She's silly too
She's an acrobat

Backflips while we play
Hack sack

There's a bee on your pillow

And this is

When it starts

It starts

Not every day

Sometimes weeks

Without incident

Has to be a coincidence Larry

But how did she know Liz?

How did she know?

There's a bee on your pillow

Closes her eyes

Dances
A circle

Curtsies

I told ya

Tara told me

Will you thank her?

There's a bee on your pillow

I thought
You don't believe in coincidences?

As a lawyer I don't
True

She's the sort of friend
Nobody can see

Nobody but me
Know what I mean?

Char, go back to bed
You were just having a bad dream

A bad dream

Go back to bed

There are more occurrences

More occurrences

One day
I'm in the kitchen

She hands me a band aid

What's this for?

Just in case

Five minutes later

I accidentally cut myself

Chopping vegetables

What's this for?

Just in case

Just in case

Has to be a coincidence Larry

Just a bad dream

There's a bee on your pillow

Hands Liz
An Advil

While she's
Washing dishes

What's this for darling?

I know your head hurts Mama

And it does
Stressed from work

Tara says
There's a bee on your pillow

A what?
No, there's nothing darling

Just a bad dream

Yes, there is mama
Pull back the covers

And look

Another time

Liz taking her
To the dentist

She's in the child seat
Backseat of car

It's going to be okay Mama

What are you talking about?

I know you're worried

Liz

Pro Bono director

Mid-sized law firm
Cleary, Brown and Blacklow

We believe
Pro bono work

Should be
A mindful choice

One that expresses

Both personal and collective interests

So rather than make
Pro bono work

Mandatory at Cleary

We fully support
The voluntary efforts

Of all of our lawyers

Impact litigation

Robust pro bono immigration docket

Represent nonprofits

Small businesses

Survivors
Of gender violence

Gender equality

Currently engulfed
In a case

Adamsville vs. Lopez

Rebecca Lopez

Obtained permanent
Restraining order

Against husband Sam

Who had been
Stalking and controlling her

Required to remain
100 yards

From her
And their seven year old son Peter

Except during
Specified visitation

June 23rd

Approximately 5:15 pm

Sam takes possession
Of Peter

Lures him
With brand new

Blue, long range walkie talkies

Lures him

In violation of the order

Rebecca calls the police

Numerous times

Numerous times

But the police
Take no action

Hours later

Early morning

Both found dead
In his Chevrolet Silverado

He shot his son

And then himself

Stressful case
For Liz

The police
Got away

With not
Protecting her son

Wants some justice
For Rebecca

She deserves it

Char
In the backseat

It's going to be okay Mama

What are you talking about?

I know you're worried

Peter is
With Mamuma now

Peter?

The boy who died

With Mamuma now

How do you know?

Tara

Who's Mamuma Char?
Who's Mamuma?

She just smiles

Playfully

She's imaginary, invisible
But she's never scary

She's silly too
She's an acrobat

Backflips while we play
Hack sack

There's a bee on your pillow

I know you're worried

How did she know
The boy's name?

She must have heard me on the phone
Or talking to you

Has to be a coincidence Larry

What's the matter darling?

A bad dream

Tara says
There's a bee on your pillow

A what?
No, there's nothing darling

Just a bad dream

Yes, there is mama
Pull back the covers

And look

One day

Lying on her bed

She's looking up

At the ceiling

Giggling

Belly laughs

What's so funny Char?

What's so funny?

Ball of light

A ghost

I don't see anything Char

It's a ghost

A ghost

Another day

She runs
From the bathroom screaming

Tells Liz

There was a monkey man

In the mirror
Behind her

As she brushed
Her teeth

A monkey man!
I saw him!

Calms Char down

Hesitantly
Approached bathroom

Fearful

Of what she might find

Would she discover
A real life person

Who broke
Into their home?

Or is this connected
To the other events

That have transpired
Over the past few months

Steps into the bathroom

Finds it empty

Empty

Not sure

Whether to be relieved

Or more concerned

Sometimes

Tara comes with a friend

A friend?

An old woman

Who can't walk

Because her legs

Are broken

Gray hair

Beautiful long gown

Necklace of pearls

They came
Across a bridge

Across a bridge

Has to be a coincidence Larry

But how did she know Liz?

How did she know?

There's a bee on your pillow

Closes her eyes

Dances
A circle

Curtsies

I told ya

Tara told me

Will you thank her?

There's a bee on your pillow

Peter is
With Mamuma now

Peter?

The boy who died

With Mamuma now

How do you know?

Tara

Who's Mamuma Char?
Who's Mamuma?

She just smiles

She's the sort of friend
Nobody can see

Nobody but me
Know what I mean?

My imaginary friend
Says I'm the imaginary friend

*****

In the bedroom

The knockings
Are heard

Through the wall

Through the ceiling

And again
Through the floor

The knockings
Are heard

The two Fox sisters

Have just moved

To Hydesville

With their parents

A quiet community

Of farms and fields

Western New York state

Had rented the farmhouse

Previous December

Margarita

Nickname Maggie

Pretty saucy fourteen year old

Sister Catherine

Eleven years old

Called Kate

Black haired

Pale

More delicate in appearance

Than her sister

Stores around town

House is haunted

Haunted

The knockings are heard

Neighbors Mary and Charles Redfield

In their candle lit home

8 pm

When they hear

A sharp knock
On their door

They answer

It's John Fox

The girls' father

Standing in the snow

In just his shirt

Wind wailing

Tells them

About the knocks

And raps

Would the Redfields
Come immediately?

Wants their opinion

Charles declines

Mary agrees to go

Teases

She'll have a talk

With it

If it was a ghost

But John

Is not a humorous man

Grimly leads her

To a non-descript frame structure

On nearby fenced plot

Head straight

To the bedroom

He and Margaret

Share with the girls

Margaret Fox

Comfortably plump

Long white, frilly petticoat

Linen cap with lace

Generally cherry

Now highly agitated

And exhausted

Greets Mary

Glances inside room

Lit by a single candle

The girls

Huddle on the bed

Cling to each other

In terror

In terror

Abide with me: fast falls the eventide

The darkness deepens: Lord with me abide

When other helpers fail and comforts flee

Help of the helpless, O abide with me

Margaret draws
Mary down beside her

Other bed
In the room

Begins to speak

Into what seems

Like thin air

Begins to speak

Now count five!

Margaret commands

Five knocks follow

Seems to indicate

Intelligent presence

Count fifteen!

Margaret orders

The invisible noisemaker

Does so

What is my friend here
Mary's age?

Raps 39 times

That is correct Mr. Splitfoot

And if you are
An injured spirit

Manifest it
By three raps

Knock it answers

Knock

Knock

No sign
That anyone in the room

Is making the noise

No sign

Swift to its close ebbs out life's little day:

Earth's joy grows dim; its glories pass away;

Change and decay in all around I see:

O'Thou who changest not, abide with me

Mary decides

She wants her husband Charles

To size up the situation

For himself

But before leaving

Pauses for a moment

Comforts Kate and Maggie

They're trembling

Reassures them

If there is indeed a spirit present
This Mr. Splitfoot
Has no intention of hurting you
No intention

Maggie

We are innocent

How good it is
To have a clear conscience

The knockings
Are heard

Through the walls

Through the ceiling

And again
Through the floor

The girls' mother

Getting ready for bed

A big bang
In the house

Clatter

Their father

Stirs

From his bedside prayer

Mustache

Bushy sideburns

And now Lord

As we lie down

We pray

That you would

Watch over us

To protect

And keep us safe

Stories around town

House is haunted

Haunted

The last people suddenly moved out

Charles Redfield arrives

Same questions asked

And answered

The raps tell him

His age

Mr. Redfield

Calls in Mr. Duesler and wife

And several others

Mr. and Mrs. Hyde

Mr. and Mrs. Jewell

Mr. Duesler

Frock coat and vest

Long side burns

Asks many questions

All answered

All answered

Mrs. Fox asks

If any of the neighbors present

Injured the spirit

Receives no answer

Mr. Duesler asks

Were you murdered?

Raps affirmation

Can your murderer

Be brought to justice?

No sounds

Can he be

Can he be punished by law?

No answer

If your murderer
Cannot be punished by the law

Manifest it by the raps

Raps made

Clearly

And distinctly

Ascertain

That he was a peddler

Murdered

In the east bedroom

About five years ago

A Tuesday night

At twelve o'clock

His throat slit

With a butcher's knife

His throat slit

The raps make

The sound of a death struggle

Gurgling of throat

Body dragged

Down to the cellar

Ten feet below

The surface of the ground

Ten feet below

Were you murdered

For your money?

Raps affirmative

How much was it?
One hundred?

No rap

Was it two hundred?

No rap

Five hundred?

Raps affirmative

The raps

Give his name

As Charles B. Rosna

A peddler

Word gets out

Around the hamlet

Of Hydesville

Word gets out

Are you an unsatisfied spirit?

An unsatisfied spirit?

Yes

Oh mother

I know what it is

Tomorrow is April Fool's Day

Somebody is

Trying to fool us!

Are you an unsatisfied spirit?

An unsatisfied spirit?

And many come

To the house

Remain all night

Mrs. Fox takes
The girls out

Mr. Fox and Mr. Redfield
Remain

House over flows
With people

No sounds
During the day

But commence

In the evening

Three hundred persons present

On Sunday morning
Noises heard

Throughout the day
By all

Who came
To the house

Noises heard

Mister Splitfoot

Mister Splitfoot

And now Lord

As we lie down

We pray

That you would

Watch over us

To protect

And keep us safe

Mrs. Fox

Decides to separate the girls

Get them away
From the mayhem

Get them away

Kate takes refuge
At her older brother David's farm

In Auburn

Maggie at her older sister Leah's

In Rochester

The raps

Break out

In both houses

The raps

Break out

In Rochester

They are especially violent

Things thrown
At Leah's second husband Calvin

Blocks of wood

Scattered in the room

Sometimes

With sentences on them

Come not in terrors, as the King of kings

But kind and good, with healing in Thy wings

Tears for all woes, a heart for every plea

Come, Friend of sinners, and thus bide with me

*****

A few years go by

Charlotte's now ten

Tara does not

Appear to her as much

Weeks or

Even months can go by

Without an appearance

Laughs

What's so funny Char?

It's a ghost

A ghost

One day
I'm looking through

Old photos
Of Char

Ones we got printed

And I notice something
In a lot of them

That I had not
Seen before

Not seen before

Bubbles of light

I show the photos

To Liz

From when Char
Was five

Look Liz

Look

Photo of Char
On her bed

Thick blond curls

Bright blue eyes

What is that Larry?
Looks like a bubble

It's an orb

A what?

An orb

She chuckles

Or just
Bad CVS photo printing
We should've gone to a real printer

Many of the photos

One after another

Orbs near
Or beside Char

In the rocking chair

Bubbles of light

One of her birthday parties

In a sea of presents

On my lap

Smiling

Smiling

At the orbs

Orbs

Larry, don't go fuzzy wuzzy on me
It's called bad printing

Sometimes
She gets scared

Of something

When Tara
Is not around

Not around

Says she sees people

Or silhouettes

Of them

Shadows moving

Features

Obscure

They're people Daddy

But I don't know

If they're nice or not

She's confused

We should take her
To see someone

Who?

A shrink
That's who
I think she hallucinates

Still talks

About Tara

Coming with a friend

A friend?

An old woman

Who can't walk

Because her legs

Are broken

Gray hair

Beautiful long gown

Necklace of pearls

They came
Across a bridge

Across a bridge

Has to be a coincidence Larry

But how did she know Liz?

How did she know?

There's a bee on your pillow

Liz still

Working on

Adamsville vs. Lopez

Takes up
Much of her time

Much of her time

Is going
To Court of Appeals

10th Circuit

Months and months
Of preparation

David vs. Goliath

Opposing motions

To dismiss

Dismiss

Why don't
You ask Rebecca Lopez

If it's about her son?

I don't know
That would be weird
And it's probably nothing
Nothing

I continue

Writing
My freelance articles

On mostly

Obscure American history

My specialty

Weird Americana

For **American Heritage**

Smithsonian

Civil War Times

Slate

Vox

American History Magazine

Military Heritage

BBC History

Even **Lighthouse Digest**

Weird Americana

Slaves
In Galveston, Texas

Didn't find out

About Emancipation Proclamation

Until two and half years later

June 19, 1865

Which is now celebrated

As Juneteenth

Or how about

The only known

American civilians

Who lost their lives

During World War 2?

A woman in Oregon

And five children

Who find

A Japanese balloon

In the woods

Don't realize

It's a bomb

Until it goes off

And they all perish

Or the man

Who may have

Butchered
Up to two hundred people

In a hotel

He designed

H.H. Holmes

A sociopath

Who lived

During the fire
Of Chicago's World Fair

1873

Operates hotel

That includes rooms

With secret gas lines

So he can kill

Whomever
Was staying in them

Or a room

That's completely sealed

Except for
A trapdoor in the ceiling

Where he starves people

I figure
You don't know

That one

Do you?

Now my editor

At **American Heritage**

Sends an e-mail

Propose that I write
A piece about the Fox Sisters

The Fox Sisters

Don't know much
About them

The Fox Sisters

Three sisters
From upstate New York

Played important role

In the creation

Of Spiritualism

It all starts

In 1848

The two younger sisters

Use "rappings"

To convince

Their older sister Leah

And others

That they are communicating

With Spirits

Their old sister

Takes charge

Manages their careers

For some time

All enjoying success

As mediums

For many years

Until 1888

Maggie

Publicly admits

It is all a hoax

A hoax

Demonstrates

Their method

In a packed auditorium

But later

Recants the confession

Recants

She was forced by money

We get a phone call

From school

Meet with Char's

Fifth grade teacher

Mrs. Davis

A plump woman

In her mid--fifties

Hair in a bun

Flower pattern blouse

Tattoo of hawk
On her arm

Char likes her

But she's very concerned

About Charlotte

Very concerned

She's usually upbeat

Very withdrawn

In class

Not social

*Like she's holding
Stuff inside of her*

Afraid to speak

Grades are starting
To slide

What do you suggest we do?
What do we do?

A few days later

After a weekend sleep over

Megan

The mother

Of Char's best friend Lucy

Doesn't want
Charlotte sleeping over

Anymore

Anymore

Why?

She's scaring Lucy

Says she hears footsteps

Sees people
In their house

Lucy thought
She saw a shadow move

Scared the crap
Out of her

I'm sorry
We have to do something Larry
We have to do something

One night

Char approaches me

In my study

Very serious face

Daddy

Do you think

I make this stuff up?

Do you?

No, I don't

I know you
Believe it

But do you?

I honestly don't know

But I want to

I want to

The old woman

Who can't walk

Says there was a bridge

A bridge

She and Tara

Came across the bridge

Later on

I do my own research

On the community

Where we rent
Our house

This town

Once a hotspot

For the spiritual revolution

At the turn
Of the 20th century

There was a bridge

A metal arch bridge

And it was considered

The gateway to the community

A gateway

I want a dress like hers

She's imaginary, invisible
But she's never scary

She's silly too
She's an acrobat

Backflips while we play
Hack sack

There's a bee on your pillow

*****

The manifestation

Is intelligent

And spiteful

At Leah's house

No earthly power

Could relieve them

No earthly power

Leah, Kate
And Mrs. Margaret Fox

On their knees

Pins stuck

Into different

Parts of their bodies

Kate

Stop it Mister Splitfoot!

Stop it!

Mrs. Fox's cap

Is removed

From her head

Removed

Her comb

Jerked out
Of her hair

Every conceivable thing

It can do

To annoy them

The manifestation

Starts to

Bang on the roof

Frequent discharge

Of heavy artillery

Leah, the roof is going to fall!

People the next day

Say they heard it

A mile away

Like an explosion

What is going on?

What is going on?

Swift to its close ebbs out life's little day:

Earth's joy grows dim; its glories pass away;

Change and decay in all around I see:

O' Thou who changest not, abide with me

The violent disturbances continue

Until visiting friend

Abolitionist Isaac Post

Founder

With his wife Emily

Of the WNYASS

Western New York
Anti-slavery Society

Remembers

That the Fox sisters'

Brother David

Conversed
With Hydesville spirits

By using

The alphabet

The alphabet

Tremendous raps

Come in reply

To the first question

And the message

Is spelt out

Dear Friends

You must

Proclaim the truth

To the world

This is the dawning

Of a new era

You must

Not try

To conceal it

Any longer

When you do

Your duty

God will protect you

And good spirits

Will watch over you

From that day forward

Communication

Begins to pour through

Manifestations

Become orderly

50

Table shakes

Objects move

Instruments plays

Drums

Guitar

Violin

Harp

What's going on

At Calvin Brown's house?

They're sinners

Sinners

Frauds

Tricksters

Those whore sisters

But I am afraid

That just as Eve

Was deceived by the serpent's coming

Your minds may somehow be

Led astray from your sincere

And pure devotion to Christ

You must

Proclaim the truth

To the world

This is the dawning

Of a new era

You must

Not try

To conceal it

Any longer

November 14, 1849

First meeting

Of a small group

Of Spiritualists

Takes place

The Corinthian Hall

Rochester, New York

Excitement grows

But there is

Skepticism

Skepticism

We need answers

They're hustlers

Whores

Devil's whores

A committee of five

Tasked to investigate

Investigate

But cannot

Explain the phenomena

Another committee forms

The girls

Stand on pillows

Handkerchiefs

Tied around

Bottom of their dresses

Tight to ankles

We all heard rappings

On the wall

And floor distinctly

Passions rise

Rise

They're always touching us Maggie!

They can't keep

Their claws off us!

They're almost

Physically torn apart

Devil's whores!

Torn apart

You belong to your father,

The devil,

And you want

To carry out

Your father's desires

When he lies

He speaks his native language

And he is a liar

Submit yourselves, then,

To God

Resist the devil

And he will flee from you

Flee

But in spite

Of hostile atmosphere

And denunciation

In the press

The girls become famous

The Fox sisters

Mediums spring up

Throughout the country

Mrs. Jamlin

And Mrs. Benedict

Of Auburn

First two well-known mediums

And in the circle

Of Kate Fox

Stories around town

House is haunted

Haunted

More demands

For demonstrations

Sittings

Professional mediumship

Begins

It begins

They're always touching us Maggie!

They can't keep

Their claws off us!

Professional mediumship

Begins with Leah

First public sitting

Followed by

Propaganda tour

Albany in May 1850

Then Troy

Where there
Are death threats

Death threats

Devil's whores

For as a woman

Came from man

So also man

Is born of woman

But everything

Comes from God

Their ankles

Are tied

Tied

So are their hands

Resist him

Standing firm

In the faith

Resist him

Be alert

And of sober mind

Your enemy the devil

Prowls around

Like a roaring lion

Looking for someone

To devour

Their ankles

Are tied

Tied

And so are their hands

June 1850

Bring the message

Of Spiritualism

To New York

Horace Greeley

Publisher of the **New York Tribune**

Is their first caller

Fearing for their safety

Advises them

To charge
Five dollar admission fee

Later

Under aegis

Of the Society
For the Diffusion of Spiritual Knowledge

Free public sittings

For which

Mr. H.H. Day

Pays 1200 dollars

A year to Kate

Interest runs high

In a single sitting

Celebrities gather

Around the séance table

Reverend D. Griswald

Novelist James Fennimore Cooper

Historian George Bancroft

Reverend Dr. J. W. Francis

The poet William Cullen Bryant

Horace Greeley

Reports in the **Tribune**

It would be base cowardice

Not to say

That we are

As convinced

Beyond a doubt

Of their perfect integrity

And good faith

In the premises

Whatever may be

The origin

Or cause

Of the rappings

The ladies

In whose presence

They occur

Do not make them
We tested
This thoroughly
And to our entire satisfaction
The sittings continue
Raps occur
Tables and chairs move
Sitters touched
By invisible hands
Invisible hands
Abide with me: fast falls the eventide
The darkness deepens: Lord with me abide
When other helpers fail and comforts flee
Help of the helpless, O abide with me
1853
Governor Talmadge
Sits on the table
And there's complete levitation
With him
On it
Complete levitation
Investigations
Into the reality
Of the phenomena
Never stop
Test after test
Pillows below their feet

Ankles

And hands tied

1857

As a result

Of the challenge

To mediums

In the **Boston Courier**

Several mediums

Appear before

A committee of Harvard professors

In Boston

Kate

And Leah among them

Committee

Very skeptical

Difficult to satisfy

But the promised report

Is never published

Never published

Years of public mediumship

Hostile atmosphere

The drain of

Frequent sittings

On their nervous energy

I'm tired Katie

I'm tired

Commercial exploitation

Of a gift

Which is beyond

Their control

And even understanding

The sound of a death struggle

Gurgling of throat

Body dragged

Down to the cellar

Ten feet below

The surface of the ground

Ten feet below

In the cellar

Picks and bats

Are at once

Brought into requisition

And in digging down

At a depth of five feet

Find a plank

Deeper below charcoal

And quick lime

Finally human hair

And bones

Which are pronounced

By a medical man

As belonging

To a human skeleton

*****

Liz's cell phone beeps

Charlotte says

It's Julia

Liz's best college friend

Former roommate

Also a lawyer

But at
A big corporate firm

Intellectual property

Movies, games, television

Music, websites

And it is
Indeed Julia

Who is
Coming over

For dinner tonight

How'd you know
It was Julia?

How'd you know?

I just do

Liz has
A new case

She's excited about

A Florida teen

Sally Simmons

Didn't want

Sunburned skin

To get
Any more irritated

Shows up
At Washington High School

With long sleeved shirt
No bra

Abruptly
Pulled out of class

Confused as to why

Why?

Dress code
Does not specify

Girl must
Wear bras

Does not specify

Teachers complained

Had had removed
From class

Dean asks her
If she is wearing a bra

Makes her
Put a shirt on

Over her shirt

Wear band aids
Over her nipples

Band aids

But that's not all

Sally Simmons
Seventeen years old

Told to stand up

Jump up and down

And move around

So dean
Can observe

Motion of breasts

Simmons misses
Two hours of class

And a week
And a half

Of school

From the stress

Dispute
As to underlying facts

That transpire
That day

General Counsel
For the school district

Admits
It could have

Been handled better

I felt very attacked

Singled out

Liz calls the girl
And her mother

Hold a press conference

It crossed a line

Dress code enforcement problems

All across the country

Disproportionately

Enforce dress codes

Against girls

And subgroups

Of girls

Girls of color

Gender non-conforming girls

Trans girls

Girls with curvier body types

It's a problem

It crossed a line

Liz trades letters

With the high school

No resolution reached

No resolution

Julia comes over

For dinner

Long brown hair

With blond highlights

Big brown eyes

Crinkled maxi shirt

Sleeveless lace Peplum top

Big hefty chuckle

Likes a glass of chardonnay

Where's my girl?

Where's my girl?

Still single

Like an aunt to Char

Always bringing her

Little gifts

A necklace

A drawing pad

Origami paper

Char come down
And say hello to Julia

And she does

Hey Gorgeous!

Look at you!

But then
She puts her hand over mouth

Runs back upstairs

Hey you ok?

Char, what's going on?

I'll see what's up

Go upstairs

Hear her
Heaving in the bathroom

Char?

You ok?

No answer

Toilet flush

Opens the door

You ok Char?

I feel sick

Something you ate
At school?

I can see
A black hideous energy

A what?

A black hideous energy

Coming from her body

Who?

Julia

What?

She needs
To see a doctor

She seems healthy
To me

She works out

Takes supplements

I am sure she visits
The doctor

She needs
To see a doctor

This is rude

I don't know
What to say

She needs
To see a doctor

Her grades are sliding

Her grades are sliding
But how did she know Liz?

How did she know?

There's a bee on your pillow

Another day

She runs
From the bathroom screaming

Tells Liz

There was a monkey man

In the mirror
Behind her

As she brushed
Her teeth

A monkey man!
I saw him!

Later

What the hell was that Larry?
Julia was very upset
Thought she did something to Char
It's not acceptable

You going to tell Julia
What she said?

I think we need
To take her
To see someone
See someone

I felt very attacked

Singled out

I continue my research

On the Fox sisters

The Fox sisters

Mrs. Fox's
Maternal grandfather Rutan

An elusive figure

Stories about
His wife Margaret

Are family staples

Grandmother Margaret

One of
A long line of relatives

Reputed to be
Blessed or burdened

With second sight

Second sight

Arises dreamingly

In a trance

Between midnight
And two am

Arises dreamingly

In a trance

Search for phantom funerals

In nearby graveyard

Distraught husband

Follows her

To ensure safety

Follows her

Arises dreamingly

In a trance

Search for phantom funerals

Next morning

At breakfast

Vivid details

Whose funeral

It had been

What mourners
Attended

Which friend's horse
Drew the coffin

And led procession

Rises dreamingly

In a trance

Search for phantom funerals

Margaret's sister
Elizabeth

Reportedly evidences

Gift of second sight

Ability to see

What eye cannot

At a distance

In time

And space

Foresees own death

Age 19

Tells her parents

Dreams

She was walking alone

When suddenly

Comes to

A cemetery

Walks up
To a prominent headstone

Sees her own name
On the headstone

And that

Of her husband's last name

State she died

At age 27

And it turns out

To be true

True

Rebecca Lopez

Adamsville vs. Lopez

Court of Appeals

10th circuit

Granted the defendant

Motion to dismiss

Finds Ms. Lopez

Failed

To state a claim

Under the Fourteenth Amendment

For the deprivation

Of either substantive

Or procedural due process

Stressful case
For Liz

The police
Got away

With not
Protecting her son

Wants some justice
For Rebecca

She deserves it

Char
In the backseat

It's going to be okay Mama

What are you talking about?

I know you're worried

Peter is
With Mamuma now

Why don't you
Ask Rebecca Lopez

If it's about her son?

I don't know
That would be weird
And it's probably nothing
Nothing

Reputed to be
Blessed or burdened

With second sight

Second sight

Follows her

To ensure safety

Follows her

Arises dreamingly

In a trance

Search for phantom funerals

Reportedly evidences

Gift of second sight

Ability to see

What eye cannot

At a distance

In time

And space

Another call
From school

Again from

Fifth grade teacher

Ms. Davis

Concerned about Charlotte

Wants us
To come in

Uh-oh

What now?

We come in
After school

Tells us

Charlotte
Is still withdrawn

Holds stuff in

Grades are sliding

Grades are sliding

Asks her to
Stay a few minutes

After class

Charlotte started
Speaking rapidly

Nervously

There's a short chubby woman

With red hair

Is here

Keeps saying Ethel
Ethel

My aunt was
A short chubby woman
With red hair
Everyone said she looked
Like Ethel Merman

A man
With Ethel

Has a message
For you

Wants you
To tell Ruthie

That he loves her

My parents
Married for 35 years
When he died
Madly in love with her

Ruth her mother's middle name

But he always called her that

Ruthie

Ruthie

Can get rid
Of the neckties now

Get rid of them

What
What are you talking about Charlotte?

Ms. Davis agitated

Upset

What does this mean?

How did Charlotte
Find out

About her parents?

Did she look
At my phone?

How does she know?

How does she know?

I ask Ms. Davis

Why don't you ask
Your mother about the ties?

What? Why?

Just asking

After we leave

Both drained

Exhausted

We have to do something Larry

When we get home

Frantic call

From Julia to Liz

Went to the doctor

There was a lump

On her breast

Had biopsy

Breast cancer

Caught early

High grade Ductal Carcinoma

Has to have surgery

Thanks Liz

For having that gut

And urging her

To see doctor

How did you know Liz?

Liz is stunned

Stunned

I see Char

Staring at the ground

In our yard

Looking serious

Blue jeans

And a white tee shirt

With the words

LOVE

I go out to her

Char, how did you know

That Julia was sick?

Because she is

You're right

How do you know?

Wind tousles her hair

Wipes some strands

Out of her face

Shrugs

I don't know
I just know

Glad she went
To the doctor

And how did
You get

Information
About Ms. Davis' parents?

I think you scared her

Did you
Look at something

You were not supposed to?

No, of course not

That one was Tara

Being Tara

Why do you keep

Looking at the ground?

Did you lose something?

There was a well here once

A long time ago

A farm

A boy
Fell down the well

A boy
Fell down the well

*****

What's going on

At Calvin Brown's house?

They're sinners

Sinners

Frauds

Tricksters

Those whore sisters

But I am afraid

That just as Eve

Was deceived by the serpent's coming

Your minds may somehow be

Led astray from your sincere

And pure devotion to Christ

The Fox sisters

Continue to give demonstrations

And be studied

And investigated

The raps

Respond to questions

Usually reply

Correctly

Answers sometimes

Way off the mark

Weary or bored spirits

Don't hesitate

To announce

DONE

When they wish

To retire

Not to be discouraged

Questioners continue

To press for answers

Until series

Of exasperated raps

Spell out

Why the devil

Do you ask questions

After you have been told

DONE?

Leah

This is a terrible damper

To us all

These instances

Of rudeness

Along with
Misleading answers

Confuses the mediums

As much as

The investigators

But such

Troubling episodes

Only demonstrate

Flawed natures

Of certain spirits

When manifestations

And communications

Are consistent

We believe them

To come from good spirits

But when they are

So contrary

We condemn them all

As evil

The Christian establishment

Regards the Fox family's

Otherworldly visitors

As emissaries

Of the devil

Or their own delusions

Mischief

And lies

Devil's whores

You belong to your father,

The devil,

And you want

To carry out

Your father's desires

When he lies

He speaks his native language

And he is a liar

A Methodist clergyman

Tries to conduct

An exorcism

Permitted to walk through the house

Raps all around

Clanging

Fails to

Banish the spirits

Fails

Denounces the Fox family

Sinners

Doing Satan's work

End's Margaret's
Churchgoing days

I'm tired Katie

I'm tired

Resist him

Standing firm

In the faith

Be alert

And of sober mind

Older sister Leah

Delivers more

Spirit messages herself

The spirits don't so much

Rap in the presence

As they do

With the two younger sisters

But appear to her

In a magnetic sleep

Mesmerized

Trance

Like her sisters

Suffers

From severe headaches

Stress

Offers soothing words

To family friend
Isaac Post

Famous abolitionist

Comfort

Her vision

Of his deceased first wife

And little Matilda

All new spirits

On the other side

Other side

Kate remains

Only briefly in Rochester

At invitation

Of journalist Elijah Capron

And his wife Rebecca

Visits
Auburn, New York

Stays
At their comfortable boardinghouse

Capron regards Kate

As the most gifted

Of the Fox Sisters

Eager to test her powers

Test her powers

In a setting

Without her family

Tested
In every conceivable way

Sleeps with
The ladies of the house

Different ones

Tested by them

With or without
Her dress

Tested

Sounds ricochet

Through the boardinghouse

And other homes

Ricochet

Raps

Attuned listeners

Able to
Differentiate

Spirits

By the sound

Hollow

Ringing

Heavy

Light

All kinds

Of tests

Set to challenge

Kate

And the spirits

Different hosts' parlors

Gas turns down

On its own

Candles extinguish

Tables tip over

Flip back

Small chairs

Pinion on the floor

And won't budge

Combs fly

Out of ladies' hair

Fasten themselves

To other
Women's top knots

Unseen fingers

Play the guitar

Exquisitely

Astral sounds

In the dark

Astral sounds

An invisible hand

Taps a sitter's arm

Charging the spot

Like electricity

Electricity

Feels like

A person

In a magnetic sleep

Being colder

Has moisture

Like cold perspiration

Upon it

On request

Such a hand

Change
Its temperature

And texture

Feels cold

And then warm

One sitter

Asks to see

A spirit's hand

To actually

See it

Moments later

Silhouetted

It drifts across

A moonlit window

Drifts across

Silhouetted

Local newspapers

Declare these meetings

Are trickery

A publicity stunt

All manipulation

By fall 1849

The invisible beings

The manifestations

Demand more exposure

Lobby believers

To proclaim

Truth of immortality

To the whole world

This is the dawning

Of a new era

You must

Not try

To conceal it

Any longer

But the Fox family

Hesitant

About the next step

Hesitant

Leah expresses concern

About the testing

The prodding

The ridicule

Hesitant

About more public appearances

An act

Considered improper

For respectable
Women of the day

They decide

To face the music

Four hundred people

Corinthian Hall

Rochester

A few of
The Fox sisters' supporters

Sit onstage
With them

Among them
Amy Post

Lyman Granger

Both respected

Prominent citizens

Lending their support

Moral weight

Gentle protectors

Many in the audience

Hostile

Expose chicanery

Witchcraft

Devil's whores

For as a woman

Came from man

So also man

Is born of woman

But everything

Comes from God

Some are
Only curious

Others want

Some sort of sign

From someone departed

Someone they love

Relief

From sorrow

Cravats

Frock coats

Tall hats

Shawls

Evening gowns

Maggie

And Leah

On the stage

Kate chooses
To stay in Auburn

Dark haired Maggie

Soft blue dress

That makes her glow

Glow

Capron delivers

An introduction

Full history

Of the Fox family

And the manifestations

In the bedroom

The knockings
Are heard

Through the wall

Through the ceiling

And again
Through the floor

The knockings
Are heard

March 31, 1948

The two younger Fox sisters

Maggie
Age fourteen

Kate
Age eleven

In bed

Frightened

By unexplained sounds

Knockings

Raps

Moving
Of furniture

Farmhouse

In Hydesville,
New York

A town

That no longer exists

No longer exists

Raps

Muffled voices

Heard throughout the hall

Knockings

Disembodied sounds

Some people cheer

Boos

Catcalls

Devil's whores

You belong to your father,

The devil

Submit yourselves, then,

To God

Resist the devil

And he will flee from you

Flee

Demand a committee

Investigate the farce

At the
Sons of Temperance Hall

Afternoon
November 15th

And at the
Posts' home

All on the committee

Agree

That the sounds

Are heard

But entirely failed

To discover any means
By which it could be done

With the exception
Of the most devoted believer

People outraged

How is it possible

Five respectable men

After an entire day

Of examination

Failed to expose

These fraudulent females

Outrage

Swift to its close ebbs out life's little day:

Earth's joy grows dim; its glories pass away;

Change and decay in all around I see:

O'Thou who changest not, abide with me

Another committee

Five men

An impressive group

Including vice-chancellor

Of New York State

Frederick Whittlesey

Appointed chairman

Investigation thorough

And humiliating

Sisters placed on table

Committee members

Touch

Hold

Closely observe

Their feet

Gentlemen also

Tie cords

Around their dresses

And ankles

Dispute

About whether

Knocks are heard

When feet tied

But knockings heard

At other times

Next day

Maggie and Leah

Held

Bound

Manipulated

Maneuvered

With the sisters'
Reluctant consent

Committee of ladies

Take them

Into separate room

Strip

And search

Both their persons

And clothing

In search

Of noisy props

Such as leaden balls

The sisters sob

During the search

But in the end

The ladies of Rochester

Find no evidence

Of duplicity

But there are death threats

Death threats

They're sinners

Sinners

Frauds

Tricksters

Those whore sisters

But I am afraid

That just as Eve

Was deceived by the serpent's coming

Your minds may somehow be

Led astray from your sincere

And pure devotion to Christ

Maggie and Leah

Retreat to the Post home

But there is

Still more controversy

Accused of cleverness

Trickery

Even though

They are now among

The most famous people

In the country

In Buffalo, New York

Series of grueling investigations

At the Phelp House

Sisters contorted

In a variety of positions

Heels on cushions

Legs extended

Feet elevated

During further experiment

Four doctors

Sit directly

In front of Maggie

Periodic intervals

Seize her knees

Through her dress

She sobs

Enough of this!

Enough!

Eight onlookers

Make them

Abandon their plan

To bandage Maggie's legs

The doctors declare

That Maggie

Makes the raps

A trickster

Virtually no sounds heard

When her knees

Are held

Or when a sound

Or rap is heard

Dr. Lee maintains

That he could feel

The motion of the bone

The motion of the bone

Kate and Maggie

Tour the country

Through 1852

Young women now

In the audience

At a demonstration

Is a young doctor

And famous
Arctic explorer

Elisha Kent Kane

Thinks the girls

Are frauds

Can't explain how

Attends
Every one of their dates

In Philadelphia

To see what
The trick is

What
The trick is

Never figures
It out

But he does
Figure out

That he finds

Maggie very attractive

Swift to its close ebbs out life's little day:

Earth's joy grows dim; its glories pass away;

Change and decay in all around I see:

O'Thou who changest not, abide with me

*****

We take Char

To see

A psychiatrist

Who specializes

In mood disorders

Schizophrenia

Cindy Gelber, M.D.
Psychiatrist

Medical degree
University of Pennsylvania

Completed residency
In Psychiatry

University of Washington
Seattle

In her forties

Individual tailored
Treatment plans

Elements of
Psychotherapy

Psychopharmacology

Examines
Char for half an hour

Has us
Come into her office

With Char
Left in reception

She didn't volunteer much to me
That's for sure

But she has to trust me

I'd like her to have a brain scan

To see if that will tell us anything

Might or might not

Liz tells
Her about

Tara

The imaginary friend

And hallucinations

Withdrawn at school

Friends won't do sleepovers

Losing friends

Monkey man in mirror

Says she sees
Dead people

Dead people

What could it be?

Hallucinations

In children

Can be

Grave concern

To parents

And clinicians

But not necessarily
A symptom

Of mental illness

Could be
Normal growth

Hallucination is

A false activity

Visual

Gustatory

Tactile

Or olfactory perception

Not associated

With real external stimuli

Must be differentiated

From similar phenomenon

Such as illusions:

Misperception
Of actual stimuli

Elaborate fantasies

Imagining companions

Eidetic images

In children

Hallucinations

Not always

A sign of psychosis

Hallucinatory phenomena

May be present

In 8% to 21%

Of all ten year old children

34% had depression

22% Attention Deficit Hyperactivity Disorder
ADHD

21% disruptive behavior disorder

23% had other diagnoses

Could be

Major depressive disorder

Bipolar disorder

Schizophreniform disorder

Experiencing

Significant disruptions

In thoughts

And perceptions

During childhood

May be related

To later development

Of prominent mood

And thought disorder

In the car

On the way home

Char quiet

But then
She says

What did the doctor say?

What did he say?

She doesn't know

Doesn't know what?

What's wrong with me?

She is not saying
Something is wrong
With you

You don't believe me

Do you?

There's nothing
Wrong with me!

The next day

We take her to the hospital

For a brain scan

Await results

Later

More research

On the Fox sisters

Played important role

In the creation

Of Spiritualism

It all starts

In 1849

The two younger sisters

Use "rappings"

To convince

Their older sister Leah

And others

That they are communicating

With spirits

Their older sister

Takes charge

Manages their careers

For some time

All enjoying success

As mediums

For many years

Until 1888

Maggie

Publicly admits

It is all a hoax

A hoax

Demonstrate

Their method

In a packed auditorium

But later

Recants the confession

Recants

She was forced by money

In the early 1830s

Their father

John Fox

Transforms himself

From a wild man

Boozer

Gambler

"Sporting gentleman"

Had had been

In the 1820s

Into serious

Sober man

Becomes religious

Very observant Methodist

A leader

In the church

Influenced

By great religious

Reform movement

Of the day

In western

New York State

Fires of religious enthusiasm

Burns so brightly

Area becomes known

As the Burned Over District

Burned Over

Rebellion

Against orthodox Calvinism

Which denies

Individual

Any role

In achieving

Personal salvation

Methodist camp meetings

Promise that human beings

Can shape

Their own destiny

Own destiny

Freewill Baptists

Methodists

And Presbyterians

Urge the faithful

To not only

Accept God

But also to

Demonstrate their conversion

By the godly ways

In which

They live their lives

Revival meetings

At which ministers

Exhort sinners

To convert

Change their ways

Shouts and whispers

Shakings

Hand clapping

Singing

Speaking in tongues

Falling down

In trances

John Fox

Is among them

Among them

But he

Cannot accept

What is going on

With his daughters

Doesn't believe it

Doesn't want

To be a part of it

Moves out

And lives on a farm

By the older son David

Submit yourselves to God

Resist the devil

And he will flee

From you

Flee

Liz gets a call

From fifth grade teacher

Ms. Davis

Uh oh

What now?

Sounds

A little shaken

Ruth her mother's middle name

But he always called her that

Ruthie Ruthie

Can get rid
Of the necktie now

Get rid of them

Sounds

A little shaken

I spoke to my mother last night
She's given away
All of my father's clothing
Except the neckties
The neckties

Just wanted you to know

Is that a coincidence Liz?

Is it?

We get Char's

Brain scan results

No conclusions

Except

All of this

Unusual electrical activity

Unusual electrical activity

There's a bee on your pillow

Liz continues

With the Sally Simmons case

Makes her
Put a shirt on

Over her shirt

Wear band aids
Over her nipples

Band aids

Told her

To stand up

Jump up and down

And move around

So dean
Can observe

Motion of breasts

Traded letters

With the high school

About her treatment

But so far

No resolution

Has been reached

Claim they've taken

Some kind of

Corrective measures

But we don't

Know what they are

We find their response

Completely unsatisfactory

I go to

The Town Clerk's office

Search land records

For the property

We rent house on

Maps

Deeds

Pertaining

To the property

And indeed

The property was

Once part

Of larger farmland

And indeed

There was

A well

On the property

By the spot

Where Char

Was standing

By the spot

Where she

Was standing

But now

I need to find

A boy

Who fell down

A well

And I don't know when

Or even if

Liz's Adamsville vs. Lopez case
Progresses very slowly
In the Tenth Circuit
Court of Appeals
If the Due Process Clause
Does not require
The State to provide
Its citizens
With particular
Protective services
It follows
That the State
Cannot be held liable
Under the Clause
For injuries
That could have
Been averted
Had it chosen
To provide them
As a general matter,
Then,
We conclude
That a state's failure
To protect
And individual
Against private violence
Simply does not

Constitute a violation

Of the Due Process Clause

Liz tells me

That she finally

Asked Rebecca

If the word "Mamuma"

Has any meaning

To her

Any meaning

Yes

That is what Peter and I

Called my late mother

Why did you ask?

She's the sort of friend
Nobody can see

Nobody but me
Know what I mean?

My imaginary friend
Says I'm the imaginary friend

Reputed to be
Blessed or burdened

With second sight

Cannot accept

What is going on

With his daughters

Doesn't want

To be a part of it

There's a bee on your pillow

*****

Kate and Maggie

Tour the country

Young women now

In the audience

At a demonstration

Is a young doctor

And famous
Arctic explorer

Elisha Kent Kane

Thinks the girls

Are frauds

Can't explain how

Attends
Every one of their dates

In Philadelphia

To see that
The trick is

What
The trick is

Never figures
It out

Be he does
Figure out

That he finds
Maggie very attractive

The sisters

Are no longer

Little girls

But young women now

No longer

Little girls

The words

Demon

And devils

And whores

Still hurled at them

But now

No longer

Country children

Hounded by jealous wives

Unwanted advances

No longer

Little girls

Accusations

Of improprieties

Kate

Slender

Perfect features

Moody

Can be sunny

Infectious enthusiasm

Or sunk

In self-pity

Frustrations

Constant public pressure

Maggie

Attractive

Lively

Lacks

Some of Kate's

Natural grace

Eyes shine

With intelligence

Warm, expressive face

Tiny figure

Elisha Kent Kane

Native Philadelphian

Surgeon

Naval officer

Explorer

Author

Eldest

Of six sons

And one daughter

Of John Kintzing Kane

And Jane Duvall Leiper

Wealthy family

Father

Highly regarded jurist

Early on

Elisha

Decides to pursue

Career in civil engineering

University of Virginia
Charlottesville

1837

But the following year

Severe attack

Of rheumatic fever

Forces him

To withdraw

Leaves him

With permanently

Damaged heart

Small slight man

Possesses

Courage

And stamina

To overcome

His handicap

Courage

And stamina

Falls

1839

Begins

Study of medicine

University of Pennsylvania

In his native Philadelphia

Residency

In the hospital

Of the Blockley Almshouse

Graduates

1842

On advice

Of this father

Applies for service

United States Navy

While awaiting

His commission

Leaves for China

As physician

Attached to diplomatic mission

Travels extensively

In the Orient

Hospital detail

At Whampoa, China

For six months

Before

Making his way

Back to the United States

By way

Of Egypt

And Europe

Arrives in Philadelphia

Late summer

1845

Naval commission

As assistant surgeon

Becomes official

July, 1843

Various peace time postings

Off the coast

Of Africa

In the Mediterranean

And along eastern coast

United States

Now he's back again

In Philadelphia

Reads in penny newspaper

That for one dollar

The inmates

Of another world

Would rap to me

In search of this one,

The deaths of my friends,

The secret thoughts

Of my sweethearts:

All things spiritlike

And incomprehensible

Would be resolved

In hard knocks

And all for one dollar!

After the necessary forms

Doorkeepers

And tickets

The knockings
Are heard

Through the wall

Through the ceiling

And again
Through the floor

The knockings
Are heard

He sees the "Spirit"

And he is smitten

Smitten

By "Spirit"

He means Maggie

Kind hearted

Warm

Youthful energy

Intelligence

Confidence

Striking beauty

Senses other qualities

Attract

And disturb him

An odd mixture

Child

And woman

Innocence

Street smarts

Passionate

Sexual

But restrained

But it's her profession

Something dark about it

Forbidden

She's a deceitful creature

He's opposed

To the rappings

A fraud

I don't know how she does it

But I will find out

Or get her to tell me

Or show me

Can't say for certain

How the sounds

Are made

But it's trickery

Deceit

And yet

He is intrigued

Smitten

It would be base cowardice

Not to say

That we are

As convinced

Beyond a doubt

Of their perfect integrity

And good faith

In the premises

Whatever may be

The origin

Or cause

Of the rappings

The ladies

In whose presence

They occur

Do not make them

We tested

This thoroughly

And to our entire satisfaction

The sittings continue

Raps occur

Tables and chairs move

Sitters touched

By invisible hands

Invisible hands

Abide with me: fast falls the eventide

The darkness deepens: Lord with me abide

When other helpers fail and comforts flee

Help of the helpless, O abide with me

Elisha's father

John Kintzing Kane

Wealthy

Highly respected jurist

Intellectual

With intense interest

In science

And natural philosophy

Family on both sides

Respected

Influential

Locally

And nationally

His father

Would never

Respect her

Beautiful

And even famous

With no real education

Forbidden

A country girl

Who claims

To speak

To ghosts

Forbidden

Not much better

Than a whore

A whore

But the explorer in him

Is intrigued

Smitten

She's curious

Like he is

An explorer

Of sorts

And traveler

Five foot seven

Intense eyes

Trimmed beard

Narrow features

Of an aristocrat

He does not

Look the part

Of daring adventurer

Be he is

His illness

Makes him tough

He's busy

Trying to raise funds

For a rescue expedition

One hundred men

And seasoned British explorer

Dr. John Franklin

Vanished

In the Arctic

Vanished

Was already

On a rescue mission

For it in 1850 and 1851

After 16 months

Little in the way

Of positive news

Some gear

And camp sites

Makeshift graves

Wants to lead

His own expedition

Endless fundraising

Hounding government officials

We need to find them

I am convinced

Some of them

Are alive

Alive

Private donors

Lectures

But still

Thunderstruck by Maggie

Returns repeatedly

To see her

Woo her

Every time

She's in town

Invites her out

Carriage rides

In the country

Calls her

My little Circe

Greek goddess

Of sorcery

Skilled in the magic

Of transmutation

Illusion

Necromancy

Lived on the mythical island

Of Aiaia

Oh my little Circe!

At first

Brings along female chaperones

An older friend

A favorite cousin

Maggie's pet

Teasing name for him

Lish

My dear, dear Lish!
You humor me!

Sends her

Gifts of flowers

Roses

Tulips

Books of poetry

Bryant

Whitman

Politely directs them

To the attention

Of Margaret

Rather than Maggie

Thirteen years younger

Than him

I miss you my little Circe!

She's curious

Flattered

But restrained at first

But the gifts continue

And she starts to

Fall in in love

Fall in love

Gifts grow

More personal

And fancy

White camellia flowers

So delicate

Like you

It must not

Be breathed upon

Must not

Be breathed upon

Takes her

To the peaceful cemetery

Where his brother Willie

Is buried

Kane family vault

Walks through the gardens

Blue Flag Iris

Bloodroot

Bee Balm

Black Eyed Susan

Azalea

Arkansas Bluestar

Like you

It must not

Be breathed upon

Must not

Be breathed upon

Trips throughout

Pennsylvania countryside

More gifts

Silks scarves

Purple and pink

Admits

He is somewhat engaged

To a woman

Of his parent's choosing

What Lish?
What?

Of course
I don't love her

I barely even know her

She's not my little Circe

Vows to end it

Needs some time with his father

But too busy fundraising

For the expedition

The expedition

How long will you be gone for?

Hopefully just a few months

I won't be able to bear it

I want to meet your parents Lish

Meet your parents

Yes, of course
I'll introduce you!

Of course!

They'll adore you!

But he never does

Never does

His Presbyterian parents

Never accept her

Never

The Fox family

Lineage

Of middle class farmers

Artisans

No distinguished professional

Wealthy manufacturers

Respected academics

And her celebrity

Is a problem

Not a place

For a woman

And this knocking nonsense

Raps

But it's her profession

Something dark about it

Forbidden

She's a deceitful creature

He's opposed

To the rappings

A fraud

I don't know how she does it

But I will find out

Or get her to tell me

Or show me

Can't say for certain

How the sounds

Are made

But it's trickery

Deceit

Swift to its close ebbs out life's little day:
Earth's joy grows dim; its glories pass away;
Change and decay in all around I see:
O' Thou who changest not, abide with me

Never tells

His parents

About her

Never

She's his secret

Dirty secret

Forbidden fruit

Gives her diamond ring

Set in black enamel

Oh it's beautiful Lish!

Has a bit of mystery
Like my little Circe

Act like

They are engaged

She takes his arm

When they go for walks

Doesn't want her

To say

The ring is from him

No

Never

Why Lish?
I want to show you off!

You mustn't

I don't want
My parents to find out

Are you ashamed of me?
Embarrassed?

Of course not!

I want to meet your parents Lish

Meet your parents

In good time Circe!
In good time!

One day

Writes her

Oh how much

I wish that you

Would quit

This life

Of dreary sameness

And deceit

She writes back

Now Doctor

Be candid

Am I correct

That you

Are an enigma?

Finding out

Enigma

Symbolizes

Developing relationship

Romance

Of the Arctic

And the spirit world

Enigmatic

You say that

You do not understand me

All of that nonsense

Dear Maggie

Very well

I am a poor

Weak

Easily deceived man

And you think

That you are an astute

Hardly seen-through woman

Managing me

As you please

I am a man

Of facts

And stern purposes

Please stop

Your deceptions

I want you

To give up the spirits

Give up the spirits Maggie

For us

For us

January 1853

Margaret and Maggie

Move to New York City

26th Street

With Leah

Ailing husband Calvin

And Kate

Leah does not

Approve of Kane

Does not approve

I want you

To give up the spirits

Give up the spirits Maggie

Has compromised

Her sister

Resentful

Of his criticism

Of Spiritualism

It's our living Maggie

It's who we are

He's a snob

Who does not have

Good intentions

I don't trust him Maggie

He's a good man Leah
And a lot of fun

Why won't he commit to you publicly?
Why?

What are his intentions?

He said he has to work things out
With his parents
His intentions are genuine and honorable

I don't trust him

Something of a snake about him

And you're too naïve and young

To see it

Kane sends Maggie

Barrage of love letters

When I think of you

Dear darling

Wasting your time

And youth

And conscience

For a few paltry dollars

And think of the crowds

Who came nightly

To hear of the wild stories

Of the frozen north

I sometimes feel

That we are

Not too far removed

After all

Not so far removed

Is it any wonder

That I long

To look

At that dear

Little deceitful

Mouth of yours

Feel your hair

Tumbling over

My cheeks

Sends her

Sets of

Lace lingerie

Many beaux?

Many believers?

Many friends?

Answer these questions

You wicked little Maggie!

Writes to Kate

As well

Stir some sibling rivalry

Dear Miss Incomprehensible Kate

I do not see why

You should not

Take half of my correspondence

Continues to visit Maggie

Please stop

Your deceptions
I want you
To give up the spirits
Give up the spirits Maggie
For us
For us
Even disrupts séances
For attention
I don't like him Maggie
He's a needy, self-serving
Manipulative little man
And gives you nothing in return
Nothing
Feelings are mutual
How is the old tigress?
Despises him
For his influence
And hold over Maggie
Questions his sincerity
Impact on family income
If he convinces her to retire
I don't like him
Not at all
He receives funding
For Arctic expedition
Departure imminent
Promises to marry Maggie

Upon his return

Promises

But wants to give up the Spirits

No more knockings

No more raps

No more games

Wants her to convert

To Catholicism

Even though

He is Presbyterian

Because it has a spirituality

Becoming to you

The faith's ornate iconography

Sense of mystery

Would appeal to her

Arranges for Maggie

To spend the summer

Under watchful eye

Of his favorite aunt

Eliza Leper

Lives in Crooksville

Small manufacturing village

18 miles

From Philadelphia

Start school

In the fall

He will pay for

Wants to see

If she is capable

Of transforming herself

Into a suitable wife

For him

I want you

To give up the spirits

Give up the spirits Maggie

For us

For us

                              *****

Another time

I see Char out there

Staring at the ground

Nirvana tee shirt

So does this boy

Talk to you Char?

No answer

Char?

Yes?

Does this boy

Talk to you?

No answer

She sniffles

Continues

Staring at the ground

Does he have a name?

Char?

Who?

The boy
Who fell down the well

Do you believe me?

Well you have

Said some remarkable things

It's hard to deny

Mama does not believe me

I wouldn't say that

His name is John

And she runs

Back into the house

But I still can't

Find anything out

About a boy

Falling down a well

Presumably died

I don't know when

I don't know when

Says she sees people

Or silhouettes

Of them

Shadows moving

Features obscure

They're people Daddy

But I don't know

If they're nice or not

I continue

My research

On the Fox sisters

How Kate

Marries a devout Spiritualist

In London

Continues

To develop

Her medium powers

Translating messages

In astonishing

Unprecedented ways

Communicates

Two messages

Simultaneously

Writing one

While speaking the other

Transcribes messages

In reverse script

Utilizes blank cards

Upon which

Words

Seemed to

Spontaneously appear

At least

That is what

Is said

At the time

During sessions

With a wealthy banker

Charles Livermore

Summons

The man's deceased wife

At first

A faint specter

Or shadow

But then

After many sessions

Full- fledged apparition

Materializes

In the room

Materializes

Full -fledged apparition

Business booms

During

And after

The Civil War

Increasing numbers

Of bereaved

Find solace

In Spiritualism

Find solace

Prominent Spiritualist

Emma Hardinge

Writes

That the war

Added two million

New believers

In the movement

By 1880s

Estimated

Eight million Spiritualists

In the United States

And Europe

All started one night

By two little girls

In upstate New York

New practitioners

Seduced by flamboyance

Of the Gilded Age

Expect miracles

Miracles

Like Kate's summoning

Of the apparition

At every séance

Wearying

Both to the movement

And to Kate

She starts to drink heavily

Says she sees people

Or silhouettes

Of them

Shadows moving

Features

Obscure

Liz's cases

Progress slowly

Sally Simmons case

Florida teen

Didn't want

Sunburned skin

To get
Any more irritated

Shows up
At Washington High School

With long sleeved shirt
No bra

Abruptly
Pulled out of class

I felt very attacked

Singled out

General Counsel
For the school district

Admits
It could have

Been better handled

Liz and co-counsel

Write letters to the school

Vague replies

That they're
Addressing this issue

New policy

What is the policy?

What is the policy?

This child's civil rights

And privacy

Were violated

No replies

Open Records Act

Send request

Asking them

To provide documents

Of other incidents

And disciplinary actions

Send demand letter

Violated these laws

Explain to us

Why you did it?

Why you did it?

An old woman

Who can't walk

Because her legs

Are broken

Gray hair

Beautiful long gown

Necklace of pearls

They came
Across a bridge

Across a bridge

Cannot accept

What is going on

With his daughters

Doesn't want

To be a part of it

Moves out

And lives on a farm

By the older son David

Submit yourselves to God

Resist the devil

And he will flee

From you

Flee

Doesn't want

To be a part of it

You don't believe me
Do you?

There's nothing
Wrong with me

Brain scan results

No conclusions

Except

All of this

Unusual electrical activity

Unusual electrical activity

Char

In the backseat of the car

After school

Mama

You're going to win

In the Tenth Circuit

What dear?
What are you talking about?

Rebecca Lopez

She's going to get justice

For Peter

Don't jinx me dear

No you're going to win

You're going to win

Tara says so

Adamsville vs. Lopez

I hope you're right

Word gets out

About Ms. Davis

And Char

Word gets out

We don't know how

It leaked

We don't know how

Becomes

A bit

Of a celebrity

In school

Charlotte's a superhero!

More like a super weirdo!

She's not comfortable

With the attention

And neither are we

Feels ostracized

Attacked

Texts

From other parents

Is this true?

That's remarkable!

Is there something

Wrong with Charlotte?

Wrong with Charlotte?

We don't know how

It leaked

We don't know how

Hopefully

Blow over

Julia drops by

For a drink

After work

Big hefty chuckle

Big brown eyes

Long brown hair

With blond highlights

Jackie O
Three quarter sleeve dress

She's doing well

From treatment

Doing well

Minor surgery

Caught early

Liz told her

That Char said

She needed

To see a doctor

And everything else

The problems at school

Julia wants to

Thank her

Thank her

Hey Gorgeous!

There's my girl!

Char walks over

Can I give you a hug?

She shrugs

I just want to thank you

Thank you so much!

You're special

You know that?

Don't let anyone

Tell you otherwise

After Char

Goes upstairs

To do homework

I know

You had her see a shrink

But I am not sure

That's the solution

From what I know on this topic

What do you suggest?

There's a medium

A psychic

That I know

She's the real deal

I've seen her do stuff

And she is older

And wiser

Lived with this a while

She helps the police

Find missing people

Visits haunted houses

Okay, creepy

You didn't tell me this
How do you know her?

We represented her

For her life story rights

A Netflix show

I want you

To meet her

Summons

The man's deceased wife

At first

A faint specter

Or shadow

But then

After many sessions

Full- fledged apparition

Materializes

In the room

Materializes

Full -fledged apparition

*****

Kane departs

On his expedition

To the Arctic

Rescue mission

Sir John Franklin

And his men

Summer of 1853

Maggie keeps her promise

Keeps her promise

Retires

From Spiritualism

Stays with the Turners

In Crookville

Studies German

Kane jokes

You can scold me

In German

Flirt with

Country bumpkins

In German

Write naughty letters

To me

In German

And I'll be

None the wiser

Advises her

To study

English history

And literature

Also asked

To study music

Because he loves

Her beautiful voice

A piano

Of her own

In the bedroom

Sing to me my little Circe

Convert

Convert to Catholicism

Stand on pillows

Handkerchiefs

Tied around

Bottom of their dresses

Tight to ankles

We all heard rappings

On the wall

And floor distinctly

Passions rise

Rise

They're always touching us Maggie!

They can't keep

Their claws off us!

They're almost

Physically torn apart

Devil's whores!

Torn apart

You belong to your father,

The devil,

And you want

To carry out

Your father's desires

When he lies

He speaks his native language

And he is a liar

Submit yourselves, then,

To God

Resist the devil

And he will flee from you

Flee

Comes to New York

To be with mother Margaret

And Kate

Avoids Leah

Returns to Crookville

By Christmas

Asks Kane's friend

Cornelius Grinnel

For more money

Likes to buy herself

Pretty clothing

Grinnel asks

Kane's brother

And lawyer

Robert Patterson Kane

For advice

Agrees to allow

More expenditure

As long as Grinnel

Puts Maggie

In her place

Known to them

Only as a dependent

One to whom

The doctor

Bears the relation

Of a kind hearted friend

Whose interest

In the young lady

Shows itself

By furnishing her

With the means

Of leading

An honest life

Not his mistress

Holds him

To no other relation

Than that

Of the recipient

Of his charity

Kane gone

A year now

A year

Not his mistress

Sails to

Unknown territory

Convinced

That Sir John

Headed north

In search

Of open polar sea

Behold largest glaciers

On earth

Icebergs

Cathedrals of ice

Kane calls a glacier

A crystal bridge

Between two land masses

Crystal bridge

Names one

Humboldt Glacier

After German explorer

He admires

They find

A bunch

Of artifacts

A gold chain

Part of a telescope

A key

Remnants

Of Sir John's men

But they

Never find them

Then Elisha Kent Kane

And his men

Vanish

August 1855

27 months

After departure

Kane and his men

Rescued

By a merchant shop

More than

A thousand miles

From where

They finally

Abandoned their ship

The Advance

Spent previous winter

Living in shell

Of the brig

Crushed by

Collisions

With icebergs

In May

Travel by foot

And longboat

Across 1700 miles

Of Arctic ice

Hauling supplies

And the sick

On sledges

October 11, 1855

Maggie hears

That Kane

Is coming back

Not his mistress

Travels to New York

To be with her mother

And Kate

A carriage

Is sent for her

But the man

She is taken to see

Is not Kane

But his loyal friend

Grinnel

Who has come

To retrieve

The explorer's love letters

We need the letters Maggie

We will have them

What?
No, I will not
Absolutely not
They're mine
Mine

Not his mistress

The next day

Dressed in a Navy uniform

Kane himself arrives

Wants her

To sign a document

Disclaiming

Any romantic interest

Between them

Disclaiming

Maggie

Shocked

Shattered

I waited for you
For over two years
I'm speechless

I'm sorry Maggie

It wasn't going to work

I'm sorry

She signs it

The next day

Kane returns

Hands the document

Back to her

Tear it up Circe

I can't resist you

But since

He reneged

On commitment

To marry her

She returns

To the knockings

And rappings

Kane writes

Do keep out

Of spirit circles

I can't bear the idea

Of your sitting

In the dark

Squeezing other people's hands

I touch no hands

But yours

Think of no thoughts

That I would not

Share with you

And you do no deeds

That I would

Conceal from you

Can you say as much?

Will the spirit answer?

In a lavish white silk coat

Accompanies him

To the opera

Sleigh rides

In the country

When he returns

To Philadelphia

She writes

What duties

Have you Lish
Which claim
Your presence
In Philadelphia
This evening?
I shall
Surely expect to see you
Monday evening
And now as
The shadows lengthen
And the hours
Grow sad and dull
My soul
Will leave New York
And fly to
Its treasured love
The newspapers
Got a hold
Of the celebrity romance
What right
Has the public
To know
Anything about
An engagement
Or non-engagement
Between
These young people

If this were

A monarchy

One or both

Of them

Were of the blood royal

There would

Be an excuse

For reports

And speculation

With regard

To these relations

To each other

I don't trust him Maggie

He's a good man Leah
And a lot of fun

Why won't he commit to you publicly?
Why?

What are his intentions?

He said he has to work things out
With his parents
His intentions are genuine and honorable

I don't trust him

Something of a snake about him

And you're too naïve and young

White camellia flowers

So delicate

Like you

It must not

Be breathed upon

Must not

Be breathed upon

Like you

It must not

Be breathed upon

Must not

Be breathed upon

Icebergs

Cathedrals of ice

Kane calls a glacier

A crystal bridge

Between two land masses

Crystal bridge

Not his mistress

We need the letters Maggie

We will have them

Can you say as much?

Will the spirit answer?

The shadows lengthen

Margaret Fox

Will have

None of this

None of this

Threatens Kane

To "publish" him

To the world

If he does not

Leave her daughter alone

I from this moment

Forbid you ever again

Entering my house

I forbid my daughter

Ever receiving you

While she is

Under my care

My child

Is as pure

As an angel

And if you are

Seen coming here

The world

Will censure her

Censure her

Kane writes

To Maggie

I will never believe

Such a ban

Unless it comes

From Circe's lips

She replies

I must either

Give you up

From this moment

And forever or

Give up

Those who are

Dear to me

And who hold

My name

And reputation

As sacred

One sitter

Asks to see

A spirit's hand

To actually

See it

Moments later

Silhouetted

It drifts across

A moonlit window

Drifts across

Silhouetted

April 1856

Six months

After his return

From the Arctic

Kane attends

A funeral

Of a friend

Leaves

Feeling mortal

And melancholy

Has a revelation

A revelation

Reiterates

Offer of marriage

To Maggie

Places a ring

From the arctic

On her finger

Gives her a locket

That contains

Strands of

His deceased brother

Willie's hair

But he has

To finish his book

On his expedition first

And he is still dependent

On Kane family money

A few weeks later

Maggie, Kate

And their mother

Move to spacious house

Twenty second street

Margaret's ban

Is lifted now

Motivated

By Kane's promise

To marry Maggie

Permitted

To have her

Own private domain

Third floor parlor

For herself

Kane becomes

Frequent visitor

Unchaperoned

There is not

A single naughty thought

In all this letter!

Through spring 1856

Kane works hard

On the book

Day and night

Arctic Explorations:
The Second Grinnel Expedition
In Search of Sir John Franklin

Completes it

August 1856

Centre-table book

Beautiful illustrations

Plans to travel

To England

Present copy
To Sir John's widow
Plan another expedition
Icebergs
Cathedrals of ice
Kane calls a glacier
A crystal bridge
Between two land masses
Crystal bridge
Writes to Maggie
Dear darling little spirit
Carriage rides
Opera
Privacy of
Third floor parlor
Diamond bracelet
From Tiffany's
Arranges to
Have her photograph taken
Like an important person
That you are
Don't be afraid
Of your neck and shoulder
I want you
To look like a Circe
For you have
Already changed me

Into a wild boar

Eve of imminent departure

Summons Kate

Margaret

Another witness

Swears in their presence

Maggie is my wife

And I am her husband

Wherever we are

She is mine

And I am here

Do you understand

And consent to this Maggie?

Married by consent

Calls her his wife

Assures her

You will be

Taken care of

Should anything

Happen to me

Departs for England

Falls ill

The old rheumatic fever

Widow Franklin

Nurses him

Gets worse

Doctor sends him

To the tropics

Hope that warm weather

Will cure him

Writes Maggie

I am quite sick

And gone to Havana

Only one week away

I have received

No letters from you

Sends back quick note

Immediately

But careful with words

In case his family sees it

Could I only see you

I would say much

That I cannot write

Doesn't respond

Maybe never delivered

Or too ill

To reply

February 16, 1857

Thirty seven year old

Elisha Kent Kane

Is dead

Flag draped coffin

Received in

Port of New Orleans

A hero's send off

Loaded onto

A locomotive

Across the country

To Philadelphia

Crowds of people

Along the route

Salute the coffin

Weeping

Weeping

Lying in bed together

Chilly dark

Too sleepy

Even to whisper secrets

Whisper secrets

Give us a deep

And refreshing sleep

And may we cast any burdens

Or Difficulties

On You

And not allow

Our minds to fret or worry

For You have promised

To carry all our burdens

If we will just give them to you

In the cellar

Picks and bats

Are at once

Brought into requisition

And in digging down

About four feet

Pure water gushes

And fills up the ghost hole

*****

Kane's family

Refuses to recognize

That he ever intended

To marry Maggie

Claim that

His only motive

For being in Maggie's life

Fraternal

Benevolent

Kindness

To a troubled girl

After his death

Maggie has

Total breakdown

Constant headaches

And depression

Drinking and drugs

Make her worse

Worse

Kate sad

About Kane's death too

Had come

To like him

Had said

He wanted

To save Kate too

So many tiresome séances

With total strangers

Save Kate too

And now

She is so sad

For Maggie

April 1857

Margaret Fox

Writes to Kane's brother

The lawyer

Robert Peterson Kane

Dear mutual acquaintance

Mrs. Cornelius Grinnel

Suggested

That a small bequest

Left for Maggie

Small bequest

Her trials

Have been

Greater than

She could bear

And we fear

That unless

Changes soon

Take place

She cannot

Survive much longer

Cannot survive

Kane wills

Almost everything

To his family

But places

Five thousand dollars

Separately

In Robert's care

But the family

Denies

It was meant for Maggie

Denies

Swift to its close ebbs out life's little day:

Earth's joy grows dim; its glories pass away;

Change and decay in all around I see:

O'Thou who changest not, abide with me

By May

Maggie

Has enough strength

And will

To write

Robert herself

I know

The Doctor

Must have left

Some message for me

And I know

You will not

Refuse to deliver it

Even though

It gives you much pain

In recalling the name

Of whose memory

Is and ever

Will be sacred

By Autumn 1858

Maggie establishes

Erratic relationship

With Robert Peterson Kane

Brings her gifts

But wants her

To retrieve

The explorer's love letters

To her

We need the letters Maggie

We will have them

They're our property

Devil's whores

For as a woman

Came from man

So also man

Is born of woman

But everything

Comes from God

Their ankles

Are tied

Tied

So are their hands

Resist him

Standing firm

In the faith

Resist him

Be alert

And of sober mind

Your enemy the devil

Prowls around

Like a roaring lion

Looking for someone

To devour

Their ankles

Are tied

Tied

And so are their hands

I'm tired Katie

I'm tired

Resist him

Standing firm

In the faith

Be alert

And of sober mind

Are you an unsatisfied spirit?

An unsatisfied spirit?

The knockings
Are heard

Icebergs

Cathedrals of ice

Kane calls a glacier

A crystal bridge

Between two land masses

Crystal bridge

Do keep out

Of spirit circles

I can't bear the idea

Of your sitting

In the dark

Squeezing other people's hands

I touch no hands

But yours

Think of no thoughts

That I would not

Share with you

And you do no deeds

That I would

Conceal from you

Can you say as much?

Will the spirit answer?

She refuses

The letters are mine

So long as I live

And when I am

No longer able

To guard them

I will place them

With you

But do not think me

So lost as to ever

Allow them to be published

The private marriage

You can think of

As you please

August 1858

In honor of Kane

Converts

To Catholicism

Gives up

The spirits again

Gets baptized

Gift of rosary

From Robert Kane

We need the letters Maggie

We will have them

Not his mistress

And now Leah

Announces

That she will marry

Daniel Underhill

After her second husband

Calvin Brown

Passes away

Underhill

Wealthy

Quaker

Fire insurance business

Spiritualist

Maggie

And Leah

Know Kane

Hated Leah

And vice versa

But since he had died

Been kind

And affectionate

About her memory

Of Kane

Leah now in mid-forties

Stout

Wears huge petticoats

Square open face

Thickened with age

Wedding

In Horace Greeley's parlor

Even their father

John Fox attends

But Maggie

Starts to deteriorate

Drinks heavily

Sends desperate

And aggressive letters

To Robert Kane

Wants more money

Or she'll

Go back to séances

But the Kanes

Want the love letters

We must have them Maggie

Or we'll hold money back

Writes to Robert

Drunken handwriting

Need money

Will give you the letters

Lives in small apartment

West 46th Street

A shrine

To Elisha Kent Kane

Lish

Mementos

Gifts he gave her

Gold pocket watch

Bracelet

Scarves

Isolates herself

Only family

Close friends

It's 1861

Kate now 24

Five years older

Than Kate had been

First meeting

Elisha Kent Kane

Has a crush

On a man

Named John E. Robinson

But that goes nowhere

Keeps busy with clients

Séances

Lives with her mother

Visits Maggie

Drunken states

Demoralize her

Has the most

Astonishing private sessions

With Charles Livermore

Wealthy 31 year old banker

Mourning loss

Of his wife Estelle

Handsome man

Co-founded financial firm

Livermore and Clews and Co.

In 1859

But within a year

Wife grows ill

On her deathbed

Promises her husband

She will try to come back

Come back

From the other side

The other side

A family friend

And physician

Grows so concerned

About Livermore's grief

Urges him

To seek Kate's help

Who is now

At the height of her powers

Manifesting messages

By many different methods

Spelling words aloud

Letter by letter

During invisible rappings

Automatic writing

Simultaneous

Scrawling messages

On cards

While speaking

The other

On blank cards

Messages

Materialize

Her hair

Black

As the wings
Of a raven

A raven

Hair parted

In two simple curls

After the Madonna style

Observant eyes

Brilliant black

Pensive

Beneath long eyelashes

Black silk gown

Gold cross

At her neck

During first sessions

With Livermore

Usually his home

Or her friends

The Greeleys

Experiences

Loud raps

Touch of spirit hands

A table levitates

After twelve sessions

Message comes through

Comes through

Claiming to be

From his deceased wife

Estelle

Promises

To manifest

Before him

If he perseveres

Perseveres

Meteor shower

Of bright phosphorescent light

In the room

At 24th session

Livermore sees

Faint outline

Of a face and figure

Faint outline

That's Estelle!

I know it is!

Form against

The backdrop

Of spirit lights

Spirit light

Kate and Charles

Meet every other day

On 43rd session

April 18, 1861

They secure doors

And windows

Sit in silence

For half an hour

Startled

By tremendous rap

On mahogany table

Startled

It rises

And falls

Door violently shakes

Windows

Open and shut

Room

Completely shakes

Illuminated substance

Like a gauze
Rises from the floor
Rises
Like breathing mist
Moves about the room
In front
Of them
Intense electrical sounds
Static
Gauze-like substance
Assumes form
Of a human
Then a recognizable figure
Recedes
And approaches
Estelle!
Estelle my love!
Eyes
Forehead
Lays her head
On his
Feels his wife's silky long hair
She floats
Away from him
Floats away
A brilliant light
Projects on

One of the walls

In the glow

An entire female figure

Female figure

Stays there

For half an hour

Sends message

Now see me rise

In full brightness

Rises to the ceiling

Remains there

A few moments

Suspended

Gently descends

Disappears

Estelle returns

Again and again

Almost becomes substance

Flesh

Almost

In one sitting

Kisses her forehead

Estelle's radiant face

Vibrates rapidly

Kinetic

Grows brighter

Even Kate

Is in awe

And delighted

Another time

Kate grows alarmed

As Estelle

Approaches Charles

Another figure

Behind her

Short, thick set man

Dressed in black

A velvet cap

Kate startled

Another session

Estelle almost

Becomes tangible

Mortal

Perfect bow knot

Of white silk ribbon

Charles touches it

Giggles

I can feel it!

I can feel it!

Hand moves

Across the fabric

Low murmuring sound

Like the buzzing

Of a bee

Soft murmurs

She's trying to speak!

Chaaaaaaaa

Sessions continue

For a few years

Until there's

A message

From Estelle

That she's departing

Departing

Time for good byes

Good byes

Don't leave me!

I beg of you!

And the manifestations

Cease

Departs forever

To the Summerland

The name for heaven

The Summerland

And now Lord

As we lie down

We pray

That you would

Watch over us

To protect

And keep us safe

During the years
Of the Civil War
Maggie
Still drinks heavily
Fights with the Kane family
Filled with
Both rage
At them
And self- loathing
Conflicts
About spiritualism
We need the letters Maggie
We must have them
Writes to a friend
I solemnly
Promised Dr. Kane
I would wholly
And forever
Abandon Spiritualism
With that promise
I was educated
And considered
As dead to Spiritualism
And Spiritualists
I have sacredly
Kept my promise
From that day

And will

Hold it sacred

Until I meet him

I heaven

Relationship

With Kane family

Continues to deteriorate

You don't treat me

With dignity

And respect

And acknowledge

That I was his wife

Or anything special

To him

I need more money

More money

At urging of friends

Brings lawsuit

Against the Kanes

Calls herself

Kane's widow

Adopts his last name

Uses the letters

As evidence

Of explorer's love

That I long

To look

At that dear

Little deceitful

Mouth of yours

Feel your hair

Tumbling over

My cheeks

White camellia flowers

So delicate

Like you

It must not

Be breathed upon

Must not

Be breathed upon

Settlement forced

Agree to give Maggie

Sum of two thousand dollars

Plus small

Ongoing annuity

In exchange

Will place letters

With trusted third party

Dr. Edward Bayers

Belongs to family

That has the respect

Of the Kanes

January 1865

John Fox

188

Passes away

Followed in August

By Margaret

Of typhoid fever

Having lived apart

For most of their marriage

Buried separately

The daughters

Devastated

By the loss

Of their mother

Devastated

Loved her

Plum smiling face

Frill lace cap

A constant

In Maggie and Kate's life

Now gone

Maggie drinks

Even more

And now the Kanes

Claim financial hardship

Halt the annuity

They agreed to pay

A few years before

She regains possession

Of the letters

From the trust

And against the advice

Of friends and family

Particularly Leah

Publishes them

As a book

**The Love Life
Of Dr. Kane**

By Margaret Fox Kane

But there's a backlash

Scathing accusations

She's a demon!

She's was his whore!

She's a fraud!

A fraud!

Leah upset

By the scandal

How it taints Spiritualism

Her relentless drinking

Stops any contact

With Maggie and Kate

Stops

The drain of

Frequent sittings

On their nervous energy

I'm tired Katie

I'm tired

Commercial exploitation

Of a gift

Which is beyond

Their control

And even understanding

The knockings
Are heard

Lying in bed together

Chilly dark

Too sleepy

Even to whisper secrets

Whisper secrets

**

General Counsel
For the school district

Admits
It could have

Been better handled

Liz and co-counsel

Write letters to the school

Vague replies

That they're
Addressing the issue

New policy

What is the policy?

What is the policy?

The child's civil rights

And privacy

Were violated

No replies

Open Records Act

Send request

Asking them

To provide documents

Of other incidents

And disciplinary actions

Send demand letter

Violates these laws

Explain to us

Why you did it?

Why you did it?

I felt very attacked

Singled out

His name is John

You don't believe me
Do you?

There's nothing
Wrong with me

Brain scan results

No conclusions

Except

All of this

Unusual electrical activity

Unusual electrical activity

On the Fox sisters

And Spiritualism

In general

The Civil War ends

Victory of industrialized North

Over agrarian South

Immense power

Now resides

With captains

Of industry

And finance

Vanderbilt

Morgan

Belmont

Gould

Railroads

Banks

Medium Victoria Woodhill

Offers stock tips

To Vanderbilt

Spirits of deceased financiers

Become popular requests

At séances

Need their financial advice

Nation dealing

With the death of Lincoln

And hundreds

Of thousands

Who died

In the War

Mediums

More in demand

Than ever

People flock

To see plays

About ghosts

And spirits

Searching for comfort

Disembodied figures

On stage

War adds

Two million

New believers

In Spiritualism

So many people

Have lost

A friend

Or family member

The Fox sisters

Particularly Kate

Were right

At the heart

Of the movement

Even though

Kate too

Starts to drink too much

The decision

Is issued

By the Tenth Circuit

Adamsville vs. Lopez

Now the three judge panel

Of the Tenth Circuit

Partially reverses

The district court

And holds that

Colorado mandatory arrest law

Entitled Rebecca Lopez

Under the Constitution

To enforcement

Of the protective order

By the police

Using every reasonable means

Adamsville asks

That the full court reconsider

The Tenth Circuit
Court of Appeals

En banc upholds

Its previous decision

Recognizing

A due process

Constitutional

Due process right

We won Char!
We won!

I told you so mama

I told you so

Liz tells me

That she finally

Asked Rebecca

If the word "Mamuma"

Has any meaning

To her

Any meaning

Yes

That is what Peter and I

Called my late mother

Why do you ask?

She's the sort of friend
Nobody can see

Nobody but me
Know what I mean?

My imaginary friend
Says I'm the imaginary friend

At the suggestion of Julia

Liz and I visit her client

Catherine Andrews
Trance medium

Office

Filled with crystals

Almandine garnets

Amazonite

Amethyst cathedrals

Chakra bracelets

And paintings done by her

Of angels

And rainbows

Beams of light

Clouds

In her late sixties

Burning red hair

From Tennessee originally

Ran a job placement service

In Chicago

Thick southern accent

Flutter-sleeve tie-belt
Midi shirt dress

With carnations

Divorced twice

Raped and beaten

When she was 42

Suffered a skull fracture

And a concussion

Turning point

In her life

When she

Became a medium

After she claimed

To talk to God

Renewing a promise

When she was 13

Giving her life

To him

Giving her life

One of
The world's most

Documented mediums

Spiritual teacher

Works with the local police

Finds missing people

Murderers

Draws pictures of them

Teaches prayer

And meditation

Runs a center

Angels Healing Light

Soft spoken

But speaks knowingly

It's not what

You want to know

It's what you need to know

We tell her

About Char

She listens closely

Folds her hands

You don't need

To tell me more

I already know

Congratulations

You have a special child

We used to call them indigos

I call them SAKS

Spiritually Advanced Kids

Recognize

That your child

Belongs

To a new generation

Of kids

More evolved

More gifted

More able

To delve

Into the realm

Of the sixth sense

She is a child of light

Charlotte is

Clairsentient

Feels everything

Feels everything

The energy

In the room

When people

Are arguing

Picks up energy

From a crowd

A grocery store

A hectic classroom

May feel energy

Over distance

Grandma's got the flu

She has a stomach ache

Even if Grandma is

Two thousand miles away

She just knows stuff

That's not a nice man

That dog is lot

That lady is sad

Because her husband died

Tough being

A clairsentient

Kids aren't equipped

To deal

With heavy emotions

We need

To really listen

To her

In an authentic

And interesting way

Normalize

The experience

Allow her

To talk freely

About the experience

Be supportive

Don't say

I believe that you believe it

No

That doesn't play well

You must believe

She stands up

Gives us a necklace

With a green stone

Give this to the child

She should always wear it

The world of crystals

Is extensive

And so are the properties

This is a malachite

Used for ornaments

Pigments for paints

I've used them in mine

A very strong crystal

Aids in the healing

Of trauma

This crystal

Wants to bring openness

To one's life

Transformation

In one's life

It also protects

Make sure

You give it to Charlotte

She is so strong
Thank you so much
For your help
Just be there
For here
Be present
Also
There is a choice
She can choose
To make
The spirits
Go away
She can send
Tara away
Tara wants to
Help her
But Charlotte
Can kindly
And with compassion
And love
Ask her to depart
Love and light to you
In the car
On the way home
Liz is quiet
Well?
What did you think?
That was outside
Of my previous experience

For friggin sure
But?
She seems legit
Formidable
You can get
A reading from her
I would be afraid to
When we get home
A text
From Megan
Mother
Of Char's best friend Lucy

Wants Liz
To call her

Wants to
Tell her something

About Char

Don't worry
It's not bad

Just unusual

Liz calls

Char was

Over yesterday

Told Megan

She sensed

A spiritual visitor

In the room

With them

In the room

Yeah?
Tell me more

Who is it?

There's a man

In a wheelchair

He lived

In this house

Forty years ago

Likes what

You've done

With the renovations

Describes the way

The house

Originally looked

Smaller house

White weatherboard
Exterior

Megan

Enlarged the first floor

Open floor kitchen

Wide spaces

I'm sorry Megan

Don't be sorry

I'll have to explain
More over a drink

We have a neighbor

Who lives

In the house

She grew up in

I asked

About a man

In a wheelchair

She said

Oh that was old man Biggs

He had a stroke

She showed me

A photo

Of what

The house

Originally looked like

She used to play there

Char was right

She was right

And my mind

Was just blown

Wow

She also said to me yesterday

I don't come to them Megan

They come to me

Reputed to be
Blessed or burdened

With second sight

Second sight

Follows her

To ensure safety

Follows her

Arises dreamingly

In a trance

Search for phantom funerals

Reportedly evidences

Gift of second sight

Ability to see

What eye cannot

At a distance

In time and space

*****

Startled

By tremendous rap

On mahogany table

Startled

It rises

And falls

Door violently shakes

Windows

Open and shut

Room

Completely shakes

Illuminate substance

Like a gauze

Rises from the floor

Rises

Like breathing mist

Moves about the room

In front of them

Intense electrical sounds

Static

Gauze-like substance

Assumes form

Of a human

Then a recognizable figure

Recedes

And approaches

Estelle!

Estelle my love!

Eyes

Forehead

Lays her hand

On his

Feels his wife's silky long hair

She floats

Away from him

Floats away

A brilliant light

Projects on

One of the walls

In the glow

An entire female figure

Female figure

Stays there

For half an hour

Sends message

Now see me rise

Although Leah

Turns her back

On her two sisters

Many old friends

Try to keep Kate

From sinking

Into alcohol

Like Maggie

Part of post War culture

And wealthy clients

Court her

With champagne

Elisha Kent Kane

Had noticed

Both sisters

Had a fondness

For the sauce

Warns Maggie

Tell Kate

To drink no champagne

And do you

Follow the same advice

It makes

Your nose red

And is a bad custom

For young ladies

Dr. Edward Bayard

Former trusteee

Of Kane's love letters

Arranges for Kate

To be boarded

As a patient

At George Taylor

Swedish Movement Cure

Paid for by Bayard

And Charles Livermore

Taylor and his wife

Become Kate's

Second family

Her rock

And support

Taylor

Mid-forties

Studied at Harvard

And NYU

His wife Sarah

Ten years younger

A former high school principal

Plump

Pretty

Reminds Kate

Of her deceased mother

Dr. Taylor

Had gone

To Sweden

To learn

Massage

Passive gymnastics

For chronically ill patients

Opens what

Would now

Be called a health spa

Water cures

Exercise

Steam powered massage

Vegetarian diets

Kate boards

For many years

Begins holding séances

For George and Sarah

In 1869

In exchange

She retain access

To their comfortable home

And treatments

Receives communication

From their two dead children

Frankie

Died several years before

Tubercular meningitis

And Leila

Died of scarlet fever

18 months old

The Taylors

Have an older son

William

Ten years old

Takes part

In the sessions

Writes about them

Sixty years later

Kate brings through

Many otherworldly beings

Professor K

Uncle Albert

Various grandparents

Sarah's brother Olin

The spirits

Of their children

Play with them

Play

Frankie pulls

His papa's long beard

Braids it

Many spirits present

Lively ensemble

Of raps

Echoes

Kate transcribes

With her left hand

Writes in reverse

Long sheets

Of brown paper

Dr. Taylor

Holds a mirror up

So Sarah

Can copy

Messages

Into her journal

A roomful

Of visible

And invisible entities

Bickering

Teasing

Like old friends

Family

Professor K

Advises Sarah

To hire

More household help

One night

Phosphorescent lights

Arise

Float among them
They were like
The dear light
Of a glow worm
Touches them
Powerful force
Slams the table
A participant asks
To hold a handkerchief
In his hand
To his surprise
Globe of light
Rests in it
A gloved hand
Displays itself
One side
Then the other
Disembodied hand
Snatches pencil
And paper
Writes a message
Then lifts
Him up
Lifts him up
Another night
A crayon drawing
Of their son Frankie

Sweetest

Purest

Spiritual likeness

Our dear, dear Frankie

Five years

In heaven

Five years

Other nights

More drawings

Ordered by Olin

But as

The sessions continue

Weigh on Kate

Weigh on her

Condition

Starts to deteriorate

Too draining

Exhausting

Stressful

Too much

Passes out

During a session

In June

Kate visits Maggie

Finds her drunk

Catatonic

Throws her

214

Into a depression

A spirit

Advises the Taylors

That for the sake

Of her health

Kate needs

Drastic change

Of scenery

Drastic change

Sarah originally against

But Frankie and Leila!

Our sweet babies

I'll feel empty

This is why she needs to go

Drastic change

1871

Thirty four years old

Kate sails

To London

Whisper secrets

Abide with me: fast falls the eventide

The darkness deepens: Lord with me abide

When other helpers fail and comforts flee

Help of the helpless, O abide with me

Once in London

Holds séances

Meets fellow Spiritualists

Not long

After she arrives

Finds out

That Charles Livermore

Is engaged

To be married

A woman

Twenty years younger

Upsets Kate

For so long

Identified herself

With Estelle's spirit

She soon

Meets her own suitor

Henry Dietrich Jencken

Tall

Fair

Imposing

In appearance

Describes him

To a friend

A man

Of *good kind*

In his late forties

A widower

But not a good marriage

A barrister

216

Edited a book
On Roman law
Used by many colleagues
The son of
Spiritualists
His father a doctor
In Estonia
Fallen in love
With a married baroness
Who would
Become Henry's mother
Move to England
But struggle with the language
Considered eccentrics
December 14, 1872
Now thirty five
Kate marries Henry
St. Marylebone Church
In London
The poets Robert and Elizabeth Browning
Had wed there
Francis Bacon
Wedding party small
None of Kate's siblings attend
Maggie too frail
Leah too busy
With her new husband

And her own séances

Bride, groom

And wedding party

Arrive at the church

In three carriages

Kate

In simple white dress

Gold brooch

At her neck

Wreath of flowers

In her black hair

According to guests

Raps

Of approval

Heard during the ceremony

The spirit of my mother

Margaret Fox

I believe she approves

Banquet table

Laden with food

Levitates

Kate immediately

Becomes pregnant

Is happiest

She has ever been

Happiest

Cuts back

The séances

Only in selective

Private circles

Spring 1873

Kate and Henry

Attend four sittings

With mediums

William Stainton Moses

Oxford scholar

Ordained minister

Keeps notes

Describes Kate's voice

Speaks rapidly

Sharply

Face thin

Pronounced nose

And brow

Tight, small mouth

Thick dark hair

Piercing purple black eyes

Altogether out
Of the common

Renowned physicist
And chemist

William Crookes

Studies Kate

In his lab

Later knighted

For his discoveries

Field of vacuum physics

Interested

In the afterlife

Not just

For science's sake

But his own

Brother's death

Among phenomena

He witnesses

With Kate

Movement of heavy table

In full light

No one touching it

Floating, glowing

Orbs of light

Spectral hands

Spirit writing

Gives message

Automatic writing

To one person

At the same time

Another person

Receives message

Alphabetically

By means of raps

While conversing freely

To third person

On a different subject

Your powers

And certainty

Of the sounds

I have met with no one

Who at all approaches

Miss Kate Fox

She can place

Her hand

On any substance

And sounds ring out

Like a triple pulsation

Most astonishing

I have heard

The sounds

In a living tree

On a sheet of glass

On a stretched iron write

On a stretched membrane

A tambourine

On the roof

Of a cab

On the floor

Of a theatre

I have heard

These sounds

Proceeding from the floor

Walls

And when

The medium's hands and feet

Were held

When she was

Standing on a chair

When she was suspended

In a swing

From the ceiling

When she was

Enclosed in a wire cage

And when she had fallen

Fainting on a sofa

I have heard them

On a glass harmonicon

I have felt them

On my own shoulders

And under my own hands

I have heard them

On a sheet of paper

Held between the fingers

By a piece of thread

Passed through one corner

Crooke's experiments

Eliminate possibilities

Of trickery
And humiliation
Of the medium
That she had previously
Been subjected to
For money and fame
The scientist concludes
That the manifestations
Are real
Real
They are facts
But he does not know
What it all means
Does not know
Does not know
If it is the afterlife
What is all means
Calls it some sort
Of Psychic Force
Psychic Force
Kate and Henry
Spend the summer
On the coast
A miserable pregnancy
But so happy to be
With her love
Nine months

After the wedding

A boy

Ferdinand Dietrich Lowenstein Jencken

Is born

Nicknamed Ferdie

Rumored to

Have the gift

Of second sight

Nursemaids report

Veiled white figures

In Ferdie's room

At six months

Can take a pencil

Write message

In Greek

Kate quickly

Becomes pregnant again

October, 1874

She and Ferdie

Sail to New York

To visit family

Henry stays behind

Attends to business

Henry Jr.

Is born

In Leah's home

Early 1875

Spends time with Maggie

Now in her early forties

Adores her new nephews

I'm Auntie M

Seems to have

Recovered somewhat

Still reveres

Elisha Kent Kane

So much

That might have been

So much

But no money

From his family

And very little

From book of his love letters

Drinks less

Holds séances

Even though

She feels

She is

Betraying Lish

But needs the money

Needs the money

Has almost

Nothing to do with Leah

She is writing a book you know

She'll probably take all of the credit

Wouldn't put it past her

She has money

And she gives me nothing

Nothing

May, 1875

After separation

Of seven months

Henry Jencken

Finally arrives

In New York

Meets his new son

And Kate's family

They return to London

As a family

Kate struggles

With the illnesses

Of the boys

Sickly

But enjoys

Being a mother

And a wife

The happiness

Does not last long

Does not last

In a letter

To his brother

In Australia

Henry writes

In my home

My two little boys

Are growing up

Into boyhood

And offer me

Much pleasure

The day of schooling

Is almost upon us

But he does

Not live

To see the day arrive

After ten years

Of bliss and marriage

Henry suffers a stroke

Dies three days later

Leaves Kate

With two little boys

Six and eight years old

*****

With limited resources

And no real reason

To stay in England

Kate and her sons

Return to New York

1885

Move in

With Leah and David

Visits

George and Sarah Taylor

Not seen them

For ten years

Sarah

My joy

Can be better imagined

Then described

Here was

Katie looking well

Though ten years older

With two nice healthy

English boys

The spirits

Are all happy

Olin assure Sarah

Writes out

Each word

We shall

Talk of the past

Present and future

We will bring

All of the loved ones back

To whisper

Their loving greetings

In your ear

Later that summer

Kate and the boys

Leave Leah's

Move to

Brother David's farm

Wayne County

Leah too much

To handle

Views her nieces

And nephews

Like her own children

Too controlling

Overwhelming

Ferdie and Henry

Don't like it

She's too nosy mother

Always touching us

But Kate

Wants to leave

For another reason

Imminent publication

Leah's book

**The Missing Link
In Modern Spiritualism**

Full of newspaper articles

Letters

A history

Of the Fox family

Thrill of séances

Their abilities

Money

Gifts

Helping others

All with Leah

Front and center

The driving force

Nostalgic

Bombastic

Sensational

They took the medium

Into a room

Bolted the door

And erected a platform

Of tables

On which

The mediums

Were compelled

To stand here

Piece by piece

They were disrobed

By the committee

Of every article

Of wearing apparel

Examined

And laid aside

Kate and Maggie

Think the book

Is full of exaggerations

Self-aggrandizement

Enrages them

Kate stays at David's farm

Until late fall

1885

Rents ground floor apartment

New York City

East 84th Street

Private séances

Public events

Kate's Public Evening

Once a week

Objects float

Pitchers

Candlesticks

Trays

Tables levitate

Invisible hands

Caress

And poke

Materialize

But with husband

Henry gone

Kate cannot

Resist temptation

Temptation

Succumbs again

To the allure of alcohol

George Taylor

Finds her

Drunk in saloon

At the bar

Head hanging down

Slurs

Helllllooooooo Geooorge!

Two year

Of binge drinking

May 4, 1888

Kate arrested

Held for three hundred dollars bail

Harlem Police Court

Charge of neglect

Fourteen year old Ferdie
Twelve year old Henry

Society for
The Prevention of Cruelty
To Children

Otherwise known

As Gerry's Society

After its founder

Got word

Of her behavior

When the police arrive

Boys seem healthy

Bright eyed

Happy

To the arresting officers

But Kate

Clearly sloshed

Sloshed

Boys sent

To Juvenile Asylum

Whole Spiritualist movement

Alarmed

By these events

Alarmed

A blight on us

The Movement doesn't need this

Damage

It is doing

Fiercely denies

She neglected

The boys

They're my babies

My babies!

Admits to

Intemperate habits

Her once pretty

And handsome face

Now lined

With worry

Wrinkles

Fatigue

Kate attacked

By the public

Other spiritualist

A huckster

A whore

Fraud!

Devil's spawn

Swift to its close ebbs out life's little day:

Earth's joy grows dim; its glories pas away

Change and decay in all around I see:

O'Thou who changest not, abide with me

I'm tired Katie

I'm tired

Resist him

Standing firm

In the faith

Be alert

And of sober mind

Are you an unsatisfied spirit?

An unsatisfied spirit?

The knockings
Are heard

Lying together

Chilly dark

Too sleepy

Even to whisper secrets

Whisper secrets

Word of nephew's detention

Reaches Maggie

Visiting friends

In England

Will not sit idly by

When her dear baby sister

Is in trouble

No way

Formulates a plan

Sends a cable

Not with her name

But Edward Jencken

Henry's brother

In Australia

Whom she claims

Is the boy's

Legal guardian

Cable orders

Ferdie and Henry

To be released

To the custody of Kate

It works

They're released

Book passage

To England

When they arrive

In London

Throws arms

Around nephews

Chuckles

Here's your Uncle Edward boys!

Hello Uncle Edward!

They shout

When they all return

To New York

Maggie fumes

About Leah

And the Movement

In general

Kate suspects

That Leah

Behind seizure

Of her boys

Maybe some real concern

But Maggie and Kate

Tired of Leah's jealousy

Control tactics

Lies about herself

Elevating her achievements

I'm going to end this
Once and for all Katie
She's acted out of jealousy and spite
Once and for all
It all ends Katie

Reporter

From the **New York Herald**

Meets Maggie

At her apartment

West 44th Street

Wears simple negligee

Her face expresses

Sorrow and

World-wide experience

As Maggie talks to him

Paces the room

Covers her face

With her hands

Sits down suddenly

At her piano

Bangs out notes

Bangs

Story is published

Next day

A Celebrated Medium

Says the Spirits

Never Return

Lengthy interview

Blasts her big sister Leah

And even her

Deceased mother

When Spiritualism

First born

Kate and I

Were little children

And this old woman

My other sister

Made us

Her tools

Mother

Was a silly woman

She was a fanatic

I call her that

Because she was honest

She believed in these things

We were

But innocent little children

What did we know?

We grew

To know too much

Our sister

Used us

In her exhibitions

And we made

Money for her

Now she turns upon us

Because she's the wife

Of a rich man

And exposes us

Whenever she can

I am after her!

You can kill sometimes

Without using weapons

You know

The night

October 21, 1885

The Academy of Music

Packed to the rafters

Doubters

Staunch supporters

Of Spiritualism

The merely curious

Margaret Fox Kane

With Kate

In the audience

Maggie

Has come

To deal

The Movement

And Leah

A death blow

Death blow

Icebergs

Cathedrals of ice

Kane calls a glacier

A crystal bridge

Between two land masses

Crystal bridge

Of your neck and shoulder

I want you

To look like a Circe

For you have

Already changed me

Into a wild boar

She stands on stage

Black dress

Flowered hat

Hands shaking

Takes eyeglasses

On and off

Reads from

Her prepared statement

Glances at the audience

Get off the stage whore!

We always knew you were a fraud

Go Maggie!

Traitor!

Liar!

Leah abused

Innocent children

Manipulated babies

Who knew

No better

Knew

No better

Liar!

She was helping you!

Boos

Applauds

Screams

Helpless

Under her

Evil influence

We know

Who the evil one was!

Helpless

Under her

Evil influence

Hisses

My sister Katie

And myself

Were very young children

When this

Horrible deception began

They were mischievous

Little girls

Who liked

To terrify

Their gullible mother

She was

A good woman

Go back to hell where you belong!

Kane's slut!

At night

When we

Went to bed

We used

To tie

An apple

On a string

And move the string

Boos

Hisses

Yes

It's true

And move the string

Up and down

To bump

On the floor

Boos

Cheers

I knew you were a phony!

These are lies! Blasphemy!

Screaming

Cheering

Catcalls

Hisses

Or we would

Drop

The apple

On the floor

Making a strange noise

Every time

It would rebound

More hisses

Laughter

People yelling for silence

They also

Rapped with

Their knuckles

And joints

A technique

Developed

By Kate

Whistles

The Lord will not forgive!

Catcalls

Listen to me people

243

The rappings

Are simply

The result

Of a perfect control

Of the muscles

Of the leg

Below the knee

No one

Suspected us

Of any trick

Because we were

Such young children

They wanted to stop

But it was

Their sister

Who forced them

To continue

Forced them

To continue

Takes them to Rochester

Putting them on exhibit

She wanted

To start

A new religion

Told them

That this

Was all real

All real

I know my dead husband

Is looking at me now

And blessing me

For my work

Spiritualism is

A fraud

Of the worst description

And all of these lies

Are the fault of Leah

Hisses

From the audience

Traitor!!!

Standing ovation

From others

Months after

The event

At Academy of Music

Kate tours the region

Repeats accusations

Against Spiritualism

Appears in Rochester

City where

She and Maggie

First became renowned

January 1889

Writes to a friend

Wants to make money

Proving that knockings

Not made

With the toes

So many people

Have come to me

To ask

About the exposure

Of Maggie's

That I have

To deny myself

To them

They are

Hard at work

To expose

The whole thing

If they can

But they

Certainly cannot

But not even

A year after the confession

November 16, 1889

Maggie recants

The confession

Recants

Pressured to do it

Too weak

To resist

Was paid for it

Needed the money

She drank

Too much

Wanted to destroy Leah

Powerful forces

In the Catholic Church

Squeezed her

I am a Catholic

I converted for my deceased

Dear husband

It's all real

It's real

Would to God

That I could

Undo the injustice

I did

The cause of Spiritualism

Under the strong

Psychological influences

Of persons

Who were opposed

To it

Decision to recant

Comes from

The spirits themselves

I gave expression

To utterances

That have no foundation

In face

And that would

At the same time

Throw discredits

On the spiritual phenomena

Leah dies

From carditis

In her home

In Manhattan

Inflammation

Of the heart

Compounded by

Nervous excitability

In her late seventies

Buried in Underhill plot

Greenwood Cemetery
Brooklyn

Followed
A few months later

By husband Daniel

Kate visits

Her old friends

George and Sarah Taylor

First time

In three years

A message

Materializes

On paper

Right in front of them

How happy we are

To talk with you

In the way

We have been

With you often Sarah

So often

And helped you

At all times

Message signed Olin

Soon Frankie

And Leila return

Laughter and play

Raps

Beard braiding

But after

Visiting a few times

Kate mysteriously moves

Vanishes

For a year

No forwarding address

Or explanation

Reappears

A year later

New home

Columbus Avenue

George and Sarah visit

Raps return

I see bright changes

God bless you now

And forever

A month later

Telegram from Ferdie

Mother has passed away

July 2nd

Age 51

Last drinking spree

Too much

Her heart couldn't take it

Maggie penniless

Lives in apartment

West 57th Street

Loaned to her

By prominent Spiritualist

March 4, 1893

An old friend

Titus Merrit

Spiritualist bookseller

Notified Maggie

Mortally ill

Arrange for her

To be moved

To home of

Another loyal friend

Emily Ruggles

Brooklyn Heights

Merrit and Emily

Switch off

Staying by her side

Twenty four hours

March 8th

4:30 am

A few hours

Before dawn

Maggie passes

Peacefully

Heart gave out

Kate's body

Removed from

Temporary vault

Buried side by side

Cypress Hills Cemetery

Brooklyn

1904

School children

Play in the sisters'

Childhood home

In Hydesville

Known locally

As the Spook House

Playing in the cellar

When of them sees something

Bottom of wall

What's that?

What's that?

It's a skeleton

A hand!

Discover

The majority of a skeleton

Between the earth

And crumbling old cedar walls

A doctor

Is consulted

Estimates the bones

Are about 60 years old

Come not in terrors, as the King of kings

But kind and good, with healing in Thy wings

Tears for all woes, a heart for every plea

Come, Friend of sinners, and thus bide with me

*****

It has been a year

Since Char

Asked Tara

To leave her alone

I asked her nicely

Said that I love her

But I don't want

Any visitors anymore

No more visitors

Including Tara

Been fine

Ever since

No more visitors

Now she's in middle school

Has new friends

Who don't know

Of her past

I drive her

To piano lessons

Sits up front

With me

Wearing green malachite

Crystal necklace

On her phone

Giggling

Typing

Giggling

What's so funny Char?

Char?

What's so funny?

Char?

Just Donna

On Snapchat

Donna

A new friend

She's hilarious!!

It's not what

You want to know

It's what you need to know

You have a special child

We used to call them indigos

I call them SAKS

Spiritually Advanced Kids

She is a child of light

Charlotte is

Clairsentient

Feels everything

Feels everything

Allow her

To talk freely

About the experience

Don't say

I believe that you believe it

No

This is a malachite

Used for ornaments

Pigments for paints

I've used them in mine

A very strong crystal

Aids in the healing

Of trauma

This crystal

Wants to bring openness

To one's life

Transformation

In one's life

It also protects

Make sure

You give it to Charlotte

She is so strong

No more visitors

Liz half-jokes

That she misses

Asking Char

About some

Of her cases

Most of the time

She was right

I wish
We could turn it
On and off
Like a switch
Just joking

Sort of

Liz gets

Some resolution

On the band aid case

As we come to call it

Sally Simmons
Seventeen years old

Told to stand up

Jump up and down

So dean
Can observe

Motion of breasts

The school district

Agrees to train teachers

To avoid such incidents

From happening

In the future

No requests for youth

To make any physical movements

Because of dress code violations

Prohibit staff

Enforcing these policies

From ordering students

To bend over

Hold up their arms

Or make other motions

Clarify wording

In the dress code

About what constitutes

Distracting

Or disruptive attire

New policy

Along with equity statement

Penned by district 101 administration

Boys can dress like girls

And girls can dress like boys

You can be trans

You can be cis

You can

Wear whatever you want

Within reason

Within reason

Clothing featuring

Images of drugs

Alcohol

Obscenities

Prohibited

So is gang attire

We won Char!
We won!

I'm so proud

Of you mama!

My editor at **American Heritage**

Loves my piece

On the Fox sisters

Finally publishes it

A year later

Great reaction

Emails from many readers

I never knew about them
Thank you

That spook house
Finally burned down

Were they real
Or frauds?

Someone writes

I particularly like
The anecdote about Ferdie
After they died

Both Ferdie and Henry

Die in their thirties

But Ferdie

Said to also be a medium

The sisters' old friend

Titus Merritt

Visits him

Helps him out financially

Encourages him

To stay sober

1903

Merritt visits Ferdie

Knockings are heard

Ferdie instantly

Grabs pencil

And paper

Writes out alphabet

Points to individual letters

Spells out

Sweet message

It's from Mother

But Merritt

Does not know

What to make of it

Not unique enough

To know

If really Kate

Dear, dear Kate

Ferdie could have

Just made it up

Made it up

Another message

Through Ferdie

It's Aunt Maggie!

Asks Merritt

If he remembers the time

She knocked

Off his hat

Knocked

Off his hat

Astonishes Merritt

Smiles

Does indeed remember

Took her to Brooklyn

Two days

Before she died

Too weak

To even walk

Needs help

Off the carriage

Through the door

Of Emily Ruggles'

State Street home

Into a chair

Frail though

Maggie is

Still mischievous

Reaches out her hand

Knocks the hat

Off his head

Brown bowler

Take that darling!

Giggles

Ferdie

I never told anyone

That story

I had entirely

Forgotten it myself

Until Maggie reminded me

Wonderful, wonderful Maggie

One day

When Charlotte

Is thirteen

I see her standing

At that same spot

In the yard

Nike tee shirt

Wind blowing

Staring

Down at the ground

Where the well

Once was

Pensive

I go outside

Hands in her pockets

Wind tousles

Her long curly blond hair

Anything up?

His name is John

Wind tousles her hair

John Kane Wright